ALL YOU NEED
TO KNOW
ABOUT PLAY

♦ ♠ ♣ ♥

Also available from Houghton Mifflin in the Master Bridge Series

The Mistakes You Make at Bridge
by Terence Reese and Roger Trézel

Blocking, Unblocking and Safety Plays in Bridge
by Terence Reese and Roger Trézel

Test Your Card Play Volumes I & II by Hugh Kelsey

Killing Defense at Bridge by Hugh Kelsey

Instant Guide to Bridge by Hugh Kelsey and Ron Klinger

Simple Squeezes by Hugh Kelsey

Bridge Basics by Ron Klinger

Playing to Win at Bridge by Ron Klinger

100 Winning Bridge Tips by Ron Klinger

Five-Card Majors by Ron Klinger

Improve Your Bridge Memory by Ron Klinger

ALL YOU NEED TO KNOW ABOUT PLAY

Terence Reese and David Bird

A Master Bridge Series title
in conjunction with Peter Crawley

Houghton Mifflin Company
Boston   New York   1995

Library of Congress Cataloging-in-Publication Data

All you need to know about play / Terence Reese and David Bird.
p.   cm. — (A Master Bridge Series Title)
Originally published: London : V. Gollancz in association
with P. Crawley, 1993. With new introd.
ISBN 0-395-72861-4
1. Contract bridge.   I. Bird, David, 1946- .   II. Title.
III. Series: Master bridge series.
GV1282.3.R334   1995   94-45165
795.41'5 — dc20   CIP

Printed in the United States of America
BP 10 9 8 7 6 5 4 3 2 1

Contents

Foreword

In many games – golf comes to mind – you can play for years and not improve very much at all. Yet take a short course of lessons with the local 'professional' and you may find that your game suddenly leaps forward.

It's just the same with bridge. There are many different techniques you need to acquire before you can call yourself a good player of the cards. These cannot be picked up just by playing; you will go on making the same mistakes. But if you can make even a small effort to read about the game it will be handsomely rewarded.

This is not the longest book ever written on card-play, not by a long way; but it does explain clearly the techniques that are required to deal with 95% of hands. Master these and you will soon find yourself moving ahead in the game.

Terence Reese
David Bird

1

Safety Play in a Single Suit

The first step towards becoming a good dummy player is to master the play in a single suit. There is a right and a wrong way to play almost any combination and that's the subject we will tackle first.

The right play often depends on your objective in the suit. You may need to bring in the suit without loss; or perhaps you can afford the loss of one trick, or even two tricks. In many cases a special technique will give you the best chance to achieve your aim. The safety plays we describe here have many variations, which you should easily work out once you have the basic idea.

1. Your aim is to lose no tricks

(1)	A964	(2)	A953
	KQ1052		KQ842

The first example is a rare bird, a perfect safety play. So long as you begin with the king or queen you can be sure of picking up J x x x on either side.

Hand (2) is not quite the same thing. You cannot pick up J 10 x x in the West hand. You should therefore begin with the ace so that you can at least deal with J 10 x x on the right.

(3)	J8742	(4)	AQ762
	AQ953		J53

Hand (3) is slightly deceptive in the sense that it is usually right to lead a low card when you intend to finesse. But here, with ten cards and missing the king and 10, it is right to advance dummy's jack, enabling you to pick up K 10 x in the East hand.

With (4), as no doubt you know, it would be a beginner's mistake to lead the jack from hand. To make all the tricks you must begin with a low card to the queen, succeeding when West has precisely K x.

(5)	AQJ2	(6)	A10
	1053		KQ762

Hand (5) is an example of a situation you will meet hundreds of times. Provided you are not short of entries to hand, lead low for a finesse; if it wins, return to the South hand and lead low again. If instead you lead the 10 on the first or second round, and West holds K x, he will cover and you will lose the fourth round unnecessarily to East's 9 x x x.

On hand (6) would you be inclined to bang out the top cards or to finesse dummy's 10 on the first round? Finessing the 10 gains when West holds J x or J x x x; loses when West holds x x x and East holds J x x. The finesse is the better play by a ratio of about 4 to 3.

2.   Your aim is to lose not more than one trick

(7)	KQ93	(8)	KJ852
	J8542		Q743

These two combinations are the counterpart of (1) and (2) above. On (7) you ensure four tricks by leading to the hand with two honours; on (8) your best play is the queen from hand, so that you can pick up A 10 9 x with West.

(9)	87542	(10)	J8532
	AQ63		AQ74

On (9), if you were aiming to win all the tricks, you would finesse the queen, playing East for K x. When you can afford to lose one trick, but not two, begin with the ace. This cannot cost and you may bring down a singleton king from West. Hand (10) is similar to (3) above; leading the jack gains when East holds K 10 9 x.

(11)	A65	(12)	Q94
	K10742		K1083

On (11) it is normal to play the ace, then finesse the 10 in case East holds Q J x x. Hand (12) is one of many positions where there is a slight advantage in playing the high card from the short hand first. Leading low to the queen and finessing on the next round enables you to pick up East's A J x x or J x x x; starting with the king would not help you to pick up the same holdings with West.

(13)	K64	(14)	KJ75
	A1073		A82

The best play for three tricks on (13) is ace, king, and back towards the 10 x, faring well when West holds Q x or J x. On (14), if you needed all the tricks, you would naturally finesse the jack, but if the aim is to make three tricks the best line is king, ace, and low to the J x. This will gain when East holds precisely Q x. Note that the play is essentially the same when you hold A K J x opposite x x x: finesse the jack for four tricks, cash the ace–king for three.

	(15)	K9732	(16)	A93
		AJ4		KJ842

These two safety plays are close cousins. To be certain of four tricks against any 4–1 break, you must start with the ace on (15); later you play low from dummy towards the J x. This is proof against Q 10 x x on either side. With (16) the safety play is the king, then low to the A 9.

	(17)	J4	(18)	A94
		A98532		J7342

With (17) the only chance for five tricks is low from hand, playing West for a doubleton Q 10 or K 10. With (18) begin with a low card from the A 9 x. If East plays the 10 you can play him for a doubleton K 10 or Q 10. If instead East plays the queen or king when you lead from dummy on the first round, you may again play him for K 10 or Q 10 (if you think he's clever enough to make such a play), but there is also the possibility of his holding a doubleton K Q.

	(19)	QJ762	(20)	A8732
		A953		Q10964

Hand (19) looks safe for four tricks – but not if you lead the ace and East holds K 10 8 x; if you can afford to lose one trick begin with a low card from hand. With (20), similarly, begin with the 10 and run it if West plays low. (Low from dummy is also safe for four tricks but gives up the chance for five.)

	(21)	AQJ65	(22)	AJ752
		842		Q63

With (21) it looks natural to finesse the queen, but if the aim is to lose one trick at most the play is ace first, to guard against a singleton king in the East hand. With (22) we noted earlier that the play for five tricks was low to the jack; but if the aim is four tricks the safety play is again ace first.

(23)	QJ52	(24)	AJ76
	K83		Q5

On (23), if entries permit, lead low twice from hand, so that you don't lose two tricks when West holds A x. With (24) the only chance of three tricks is to lead low from dummy on the first round. If the queen holds, follow with ace and another, playing East for an original K x or K x x.

3.   Your aim is to lose not more than two tricks

(25)	5	(26)	KJ10862
	AJ10742		5

With (25) the natural play for five tricks is low to the jack, playing East for K Q x. But if you can afford to lose two tricks, play ace and a low card. This wins against any 3–3 division, obviously, also when either opponent holds a doubleton Q x or K x. With (26) a finesse of the jack cannot gain. Instead, play to the king and return a *low* card, gaining when either defender holds Q x or when West holds A x.

(27)	852	(28)	J843
	KQ743		Q7652

On (27), if you can afford to lose two tricks, nothing is gained by leading low to the king–queen. West may hold a singleton ace, so the safety play is low from both hands on the first round. On (28) you have to consider which opponent is more likely to hold three to an honour or A K x. For example, if East has bid 1NT be sure to start with a low card from your own hand, so that your queen won't lose to a singleton honour with West.

2

Planning a Trump Contract

There are two main ways to dispose of surplus losers in a trump contract – you can ruff them or you can discard them. It's not *quite* so simple as that, of course, and we start by looking at some of the techniques involved in ruffing losers.

When to ruff high

Some players recognise the need to ruff high only after they have just gone down in a contract.

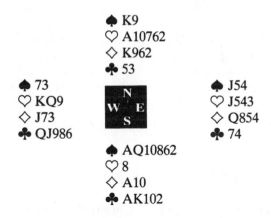

```
              ♠ K9
              ♡ A10762
              ◇ K962
              ♣ 53
♠ 73                        ♠ J54
♡ KQ9          N            ♡ J543
◇ J73        W   E          ◇ Q854
♣ QJ986        S            ♣ 74
              ♠ AQ10862
              ♡ 8
              ◇ A10
              ♣ AK102
```

South arrives in six spades and West leads ♡K. Providing trumps are 3–2, declarer needs only to dispose of one of his club losers. He wins the heart lead with the ace, cashes the top two clubs and ruffs a third round with the 9. Calamity! East overruffs and returns a trump. Declarer has no way to dispose of his remaining small club and goes one down.

South was unlucky, but careless also. He should have ruffed the first club with the king. He could then return to the diamond ace and ruff the last club with the 9. No matter if this were overruffed; his own trumps would then be good enough to draw the remainder.

Swapping one ruff for another

As with skinning a cat, there is more than one way to avert an overruff.

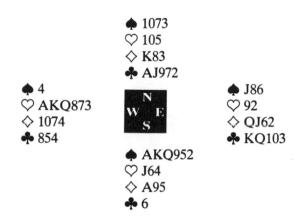

♠ 1073
♥ 105
♦ K83
♣ AJ972

♠ 4
♥ AKQ873
♦ 1074
♣ 854

♠ J86
♥ 92
♦ QJ62
♣ KQ103

♠ AKQ952
♥ J64
♦ A95
♣ 6

West opens with a weak two in hearts and you arrive in four spades on the South cards. West leads the top three hearts and you must decide what card to play from dummy on the third round.

One possibility is to ruff with the 10, hoping to escape an overruff. No-one would sympathise when East overruffed, because there is a better chance available. Simply discard a diamond from dummy on the third heart. Unless East started with three or fewer diamonds you will be able to ruff a diamond in dummy for your tenth trick. You exchange a doomed heart ruff for a more promising diamond ruff.

The right time to draw trumps

Sometimes it may seem prudent to draw a round or two of trumps before taking your ruffs, but this may allow a defender to draw dummy's last trump.

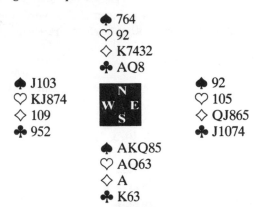

♠ 764
♡ 92
◇ K7432
♣ AQ8

♠ J103
♡ KJ874
◇ 109
♣ 952

♠ 92
♡ 105
◇ QJ865
♣ J1074

♠ AKQ85
♡ AQ63
◇ A
♣ K63

South reaches six spades and West leads ◇10, won by the ace. Declarer sees that one heart will go away on ◇K, but if a finesse of ♡Q loses he will need to ruff a heart in dummy. Should he draw two rounds of trumps at this stage? No, because if the heart finesse does lose West may then be able to draw a third round of trumps.

After at most one round of trumps declarer crosses to dummy with a club and takes a heart finesse, which fails. West plays a second diamond, won in the dummy, and declarer discards a heart. This is the moment to draw a second round of trumps, gaining handsomely when, as here, a defender who is short in hearts started with only two trumps.

Sometimes it is not so easy for declarer to control how many rounds of trumps are drawn.

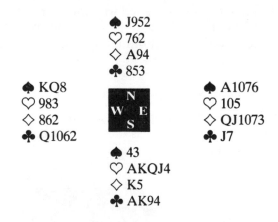

♠ J952
♡ 762
◇ A94
♣ 853

♠ KQ8
♡ 983
◇ 862
♣ Q1062

♠ A1076
♡ 105
◇ QJ1073
♣ J7

♠ 43
♡ AKQJ4
◇ K5
♣ AK94

You reach four hearts on the South cards and the defenders play three rounds of spades. You ruff the third round and see that unless clubs are 3–3 you will need to ruff the fourth round in dummy. You should aim to do this at a time when exactly two rounds of trumps have been drawn, in the hope that (as in the previous hand) the defender who is short in clubs does not hold the outstanding trump. How can this be accomplished, though?

Suppose you draw two rounds of trumps, then play ace, king and another club. This line is certain to fail when clubs are 4–2 or worse. The defender who wins the third round of clubs will be able either to remove dummy's last trump or give his partner an overruff.

If you haven't seen the idea before, the winning play may come as a slight surprise. You must duck the *first* round of clubs. You can then win the return, draw just two rounds of trumps, then play ace, king and another club. Here your play will be rewarded.

Reversing the dummy

In all the preceding deals the ruffs were taken in the short trump holding. That is generally the way, since a ruff with the short holding will give you an extra trick. Sometimes, however, you can take more than one ruff in the long trump hand, gaining an extra trick by transforming the long hand into the short hand. This is the familiar process known as reverse dummy play.

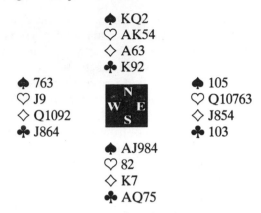

♠ KQ2
♡ AK54
◇ A63
♣ K92

♠ 763
♡ J9
◇ Q1092
♣ J864

♠ 105
♡ Q10763
◇ J854
♣ 103

♠ AJ984
♡ 82
◇ K7
♣ AQ75

You play in seven spades and receive a trump lead to the 10 and jack. If you play to set up your own hand you must hope for clubs 3–3 (or that you can draw two rounds of trumps and ruff the fourth round of clubs). There is a better way to play the hand.

You should start by cashing ♡AK and ruffing a heart high. Then return to dummy with the king of trumps, finding that the suit is 3–2. A second high heart ruff is followed by the king and ace of diamonds and a diamond ruff with the last trump. Now you can cross to ♣K, draw the last trump (discarding that fourth club) and claim.

Count the tricks you have made. Seven top winners in the side suits and *six* tricks in trumps (three in the dummy, in effect, and three ruffs in the South hand). You have successfully reversed the dummy. On this deal the play would not have been possible if one of the defenders had held four trumps. That's why, in the line we described, declarer tested the trump suit before committing himself with a second ruff in the South hand.

There is another situation where ruffing in the long trump hand can be profitable; this is when the trumps that you score would otherwise be losers.

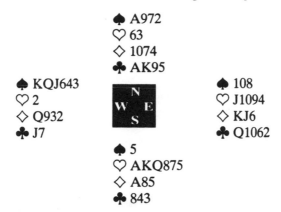

♠ A972
♡ 63
◇ 1074
♣ AK95

♠ KQJ643
♡ 2
◇ Q932
♣ J7

♠ 108
♡ J1094
◇ KJ6
♣ Q1062

♠ 5
♡ AKQ875
◇ A85
♣ 843

Against four hearts West leads ♠K, won by the ace. Suppose you try to draw trumps now, finding there is a loser there. You will then have to duck a club, hoping that the suit is 3–3 and will give you a discard. No luck . . . one down.

Rewind the tape back to trick 2 and see the effect of ruffing a spade in the long trump hand. Now when two rounds of trumps reveal a loser in that suit you can aim to score all three of your small trumps. You simply ruff dummy's two remaining spades, using the top clubs as entries. (If East ruffs in at any stage you discard a loser.) Four side-suit winners plus six trump tricks in the South hand bring the total to ten.

Cross-ruffing

When both declarer's hand and the dummy contain a shortage the best idea may be to take several ruffs in each hand, never actually drawing trumps. This form of play, a cross-ruff, contains many pitfalls for the unwary.

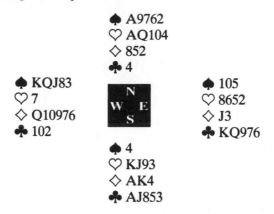

♠ A9762
♡ AQ104
◇ 852
♣ 4

♠ KQJ83
♡ 7
◇ Q10976
♣ 102

♠ 105
♡ 8652
◇ J3
♣ KQ976

♠ 4
♡ KJ93
◇ AK4
♣ AJ853

Against six hearts West leads ♠K, taken in the dummy. When this hand was played, declarer noted that he had four side-suit winners; if he could score all eight trumps separately, on a cross-ruff, this would bring the total to twelve.

The early play went well enough. Spade ruff low, ace of clubs, club ruff low. Now disaster struck. When declarer led a third round of spades from dummy, East discarded a diamond. It was no longer possible for South to score two diamond tricks and he went one down.

On this deal declarer broke a golden rule in cross-ruff play: *cash your side suit winners first.* Had he started by putting his four side suit winners safely in the bag, there would have been no problem in adding eight trump tricks to them.

There is another important rule: when you can afford to ruff high in the course of a cross-ruff, don't risk an overruff. For example, suppose you hold such as K Q 8 opposite A J 9 7 4 in the trump suit. If you can afford to lose a trick to the 10 you should cross-ruff with the K–Q and the A–J. It may be vital to avoid a possible overruff and a trump return.

Establishing side suits

So much for taking ruffs. Let's move on to some of the techniques needed when you are establishing a long suit in the dummy.

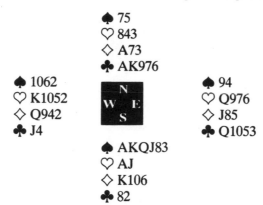

♠ 75
♡ 843
◇ A73
♣ AK976

♠ 1062
♡ K1052
◇ Q942
♣ J4

♠ 94
♡ Q976
◇ J85
♣ Q1053

♠ AKQJ83
♡ AJ
◇ K106
♣ 82

Imagine first that you take too optimistic a view of your hand and end in seven spades. West leads a trump. There's no problem about how to play it, anyway; the only chance is to find clubs 3–3. You draw trumps, play the ace–king of clubs and ruff a club, wincing when West shows out.

Now let's say that you end in six spades, West again leading a trump. Playing in six, you need only three tricks from the club suit. You should draw trumps and *duck the first round of clubs*. You can then win the return, cross to the ace of clubs and ruff a club. The diamond ace will provide an entry to the thirteenth club.

We'll end the chapter with a small problem hand, not dissimilar from the preceding deal. You are in six hearts and West leads ♠Q.

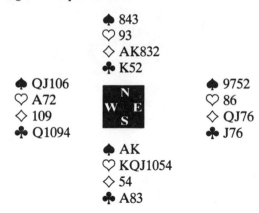

♠ 843
♡ 93
◇ AK832
♣ K52

♠ QJ106
♡ A72
◇ 109
♣ Q1094

♠ 9752
♡ 86
◇ QJ76
♣ J76

♠ AK
♡ KQJ1054
◇ 54
♣ A83

Suppose you win the spade lead and proceed to draw trumps immediately. You will then need to find diamonds 3–3. On a sunny day you might be lucky; not today, though.

How about testing the diamonds before drawing trumps? You cash the ace–king and ruff a diamond high, West showing out. Now you need an extra entry to dummy to ruff the last diamond good. If West has the ace of trumps, dummy's 9 will provide an entry! So you lead a low trump towards dummy. Whether or not West plays his ace on this trick, you will be able to establish a long diamond and reach it with the king of clubs.

Against opponents of a modest standard you might be tempted to lead the king of trumps, rather than low to the 9. If the defender with the ace failed to hold up you would gain access to the 9 whichever side the ace was. Such a play is not entitled to succeed but it's a good salesman who knows his customers!

3

Planning a No-trump Contract

No-trump contracts are often a race between the two sides. You have to make nine tricks, by means fair or foul, before the enemy can make five. In this chapter we look at various questions you may have to ask yourself. Should you hold up your stopper(s) in the enemy suit? Which of your own suits should you attack first? How can you develop a suit without allowing the dangerous defender into the lead?

When to hold up

One of the first tactical moves that a bridge player learns is the hold-up of winning cards. In the days of whist (where no dummy was exposed) it was fairly normal for a player who held an ace, especially in fourth hand, to win at the first opportunity and then look round for other fields to conquer. No longer. Anyone past the beginner's stage would hold up on a deal of this kind:

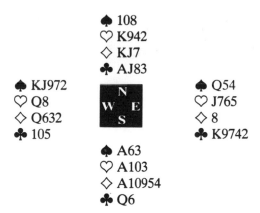

West leads ♠7 against South's 3NT and East plays the queen. Since this suit is his principal weakness the declarer must hold up his ace until the third round.

From then on it is quite safe to lose the lead to East. The best play is to run ◇10 on the first round, because if East is able to win with the queen game will be safe. South will lose at most two spades, one diamond and one club.

As the cards lie on this occasion, the diamond 10 holds and a finesse of dummy's jack follows. South is on the way now to making at least one spade, two hearts, five diamonds and two clubs – or just one club if he is nervous and no spade has been thrown. (It is *just* possible that East, not West, has the long spades.)

When not to hold up

The hold-up was obvious on the previous deal because West was likely to hold long spades and it would be calamitous to let East win a diamond trick at the moment when he might be able to return a spade. However, it is a mistake to fall into the *habit* of holding up. Sometimes you will know that if the defender with the long suit has the critical entry card you will be doomed whatever you do. Then it may be pointless – or worse than pointless – to hold up.

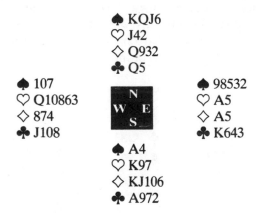

Against 3NT West leads a low heart, won by his partner's ace. Back comes ♡5. Now many players, from force of habit more than anything else, would play the 9, holding up the king. You can see where this leads. West, in with ♡Q, will realise that there is no future in hearts and will try ♣J. After this beginning the defenders can scarcely fail to make two tricks in hearts, two in clubs, and ♦A.

South's hold-up in hearts could not possibly be right. If the diamond ace lay in the same hand as five hearts, the contract was doomed; if it lay with the doubleton heart, or hearts were 4–3, declarer could assure the contract by winning the second heart.

As it happens, West had a fairly obvious club switch, but if he had held something less attractive such as J 8 3 it would still have been correct play to try a low club.

Holding up with K Q or K J

Sometimes you will need to hold up, not with an ace, but with a K Q combination.

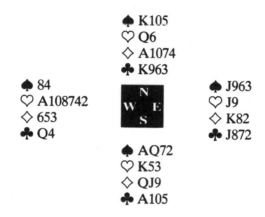

```
                    ♠ K105
                    ♡ Q6
                    ♦ A1074
                    ♣ K963
      ♠ 84                        ♠ J963
      ♡ A108742    N             ♡ J9
      ♦ 653      W   E           ♦ K82
      ♣ Q4         S             ♣ J872
                    ♠ AQ72
                    ♡ K53
                    ♦ QJ9
                    ♣ A105
```

Again you are in 3NT and West begins with his fourth best heart. All depends on how you play to this trick. If you go up with dummy's queen of hearts East, it is charitable to assume, will unblock the jack. When the diamond finesse subsequently loses you will be exposed to the loss of five heart tricks.

Another way to spoil your chances is to play low from dummy and head the jack of hearts with the king. Instead you must allow the jack of hearts to hold. East may clear the suit but this will be the end of the affair.

For psychological reasons it is a trifle more difficult to hold up when the cards in your own hand are K Q x or K J x.

```
                    ♠ A108
                    ♡ KJ3
                    ◇ 973
                    ♣ A976
  ♠ Q74                           ♠ J9632
  ♡ 94          ┌─────────┐       ♡ Q105
  ◇ A10542      │   N     │       ◇ Q6
  ♣ J85         │ W   E   │       ♣ Q102
                │   S     │
                └─────────┘
                    ♠ K5
                    ♡ A8762
                    ◇ KJ8
                    ♣ K43
```

Again you are in 3NT and West leads a low diamond to the queen. It may be tempting to extinguish this with the king and, with a sudden rush of adventure, play ace, king and another heart. This would be all right if East held ♡ Q x, or if West held ♡ Q x or ♡ Q x x. As the cards lie, though, East would win the third round of hearts and the defenders would cash four diamond tricks in quick time. Since it is easier to keep West out of the lead when you develop the hearts, you should hold off the first diamond. The defenders will doubtless persist with diamonds but East will have no diamond left when he takes his heart trick (if he did have a diamond that suit would have broken 4–3 and the contract would be safe).

Holding up with two controls

There are many occasions when a declarer who has a double stop in the suit led will need to hold up, either on the first or the second round. Before holding up on the first round he must consider whether a switch to another suit might be dangerous.

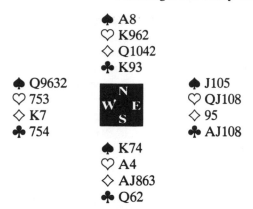

♠ A8
♡ K962
◇ Q1042
♣ K93

♠ Q9632
♡ 753
◇ K7
♣ 754

♠ J105
♡ QJ108
◇ 95
♣ AJ108

♠ K74
♡ A4
◇ AJ863
♣ Q62

In a team-of-four match West led ♠3 against 3NT and South ducked the first trick. East switched smartly to ♡Q. South won in the dummy and ran the diamond queen, losing to West's king. West pressed on in hearts and South was now a trick short. He lost a spade, two hearts, a diamond, and ♣A.

Since declarer's first play was going to be a finesse into the West hand there was no point in holding off the first spade trick. At the other table South took the first spade in dummy and ran the diamond queen. The next spade was ducked and declarer could now establish a ninth trick in clubs.

This is the other type, where the declarer who has a double stop is well advised to hold off the first round.

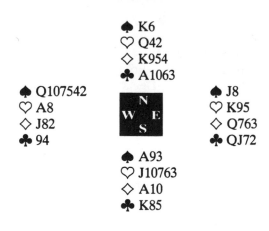

♠ K6
♡ Q42
◇ K954
♣ A1063

♠ Q107542
♡ A8
◇ J82
♣ 94

♠ J8
♡ K95
◇ Q763
♣ QJ72

♠ A93
♡ J10763
◇ A10
♣ K85

South opened 1NT and was raised to 3NT, the heart fit never coming to light. When West led a spade South went up with the king in dummy and led a low heart, hoping to lose this trick to West. This line would have succeeded against most opponents, but East made the fine play of the king of hearts to protect partner's most likely entry card. A second spade from his side spelt immediate ruin for declarer.

This time South should have ducked the first round of spades. East would then have no spade to play when he took his heart winner.

Attacking the right suit first

When tricks need to be established in more than one suit it is usually right to attack first the suit where the danger hand may hold an entry.

♠ A102
♡ KJ
◇ 843
♣ AJ954

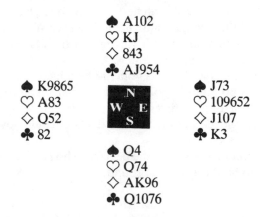

♠ K9865   ♠ J73
♡ A83   ♡ 109652
◇ Q52   ◇ J107
♣ 82   ♣ K3

♠ Q4
♡ Q74
◇ AK96
♣ Q1076

After a 1NT–3NT auction West leads ♣6, dummy playing low. East, who can expect declarer to hold one of the top spades, defends well by withholding the jack. Declarer wins with the spade queen and must consider what to do next.

If he takes the club finesse now he will end with only eight tricks; the defenders will clear the spades and West holds ♡A as an entry. A better idea is to play first on hearts, the suit where West may hold an entry. If West takes the ace, declarer will hold up on the second round of spades and can later take the club finesse in safety. If instead West ducks the first round of hearts, declarer will switch smartly to the club suit.

Avoidance play

Sometimes it is not quite enough to choose the right suit to play on. You must play this suit in such a way that the defenders will have to pay a high price if they wish to capture the first round. This deal is slightly more tricky than the last:

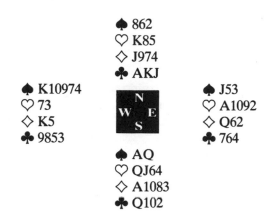

```
                    ♠ 862
                    ♡ K85
                    ◇ J974
                    ♣ AKJ
   ♠ K10974          N            ♠ J53
   ♡ 73          W       E        ♡ A1092
   ◇ K5              S            ◇ Q62
   ♣ 9853                         ♣ 764
                    ♠ AQ
                    ♡ QJ64
                    ◇ A1083
                    ♣ Q102
```

South opens 1♡ and with no bidding from the opponents arrives in 3NT. West's ♠10 lead is won by the queen. With the spades 5–3 declarer is doomed to failure if he plays on diamonds first. He will fare no better if his initial move is a heart to the king and ace; hearts are not 3–3 and he will have only eight tricks.

Declarer should aim to play a low heart through the player who holds the ace. Here it is fairly likely that West has five spades. Since West did not overcall 1♠ declarer may be inclined to place ♡A with East. The winning play is to cross to dummy with a club at trick 2 and lead a low heart from dummy. If East rises, he will pay too high a price for the privilege; declarer will have three heart tricks, enough for game. If instead East ducks, the declarer will cross to dummy once more with a club and play on diamonds, finessing twice in the suit to bring his total to nine tricks.

The Rule of Eleven

When the opening lead is fourth best, declarer (and the defender in the third seat) can make use of the famous 'Rule of Eleven':

Subtract the spot-card led from 11. The result is the number of cards higher than the one led that the other three players hold.

This is best understood from an example:

$$\heartsuit \text{ AKJ2}$$
$$\heartsuit \text{ Q10873} \qquad\qquad \heartsuit \text{ 5}$$
$$\heartsuit \text{ 964}$$

West leads ♡7 against a no-trump contract. Declarer subtracts 7 from 11, discovering that North, East and South have four cards higher than the lead between them. All of these are before his eyes, so he plays low from the dummy, scoring four tricks in the suit.

The defender in the third seat, too, can take advantage of this rule.

$$\spadesuit \text{ AQ3}$$
$$\spadesuit \text{ J876} \qquad\qquad \spadesuit \text{ K1092}$$
$$\spadesuit \text{ 54}$$

Here West leads ♠6. East calculates that the other three players have five cards higher than the lead between them. All five are on display, leaving declarer with none. East therefore plays the 2 on the first round, allowing a surprised West to continue his attack on dummy's tenace.

When dummy should play high

The link between the defenders' hands can sometimes be broken by rising with a high card from dummy at trick 1. This deal is typical.

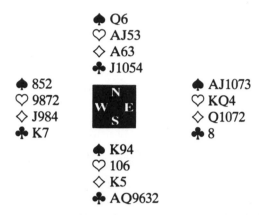

East opens 1♠ and South arrives in 3NT. West leads ♠8 and you can see what will happen if declarer plays low in the dummy. East will put on the 10 and it will do declarer no good to duck; East will simply return a low spade, retaining his ace as an entry. Instead declarer should play dummy's queen on the first trick. If East ducks, declarer will score two spade tricks; if East captures, declarer can duck the next round of spades and the link between the defenders will be broken.

Playing high from dummy can be effective in this situation, too:

$$\heartsuit \text{K}107$$
$$\heartsuit 63 \qquad \qquad \heartsuit \text{AJ}982$$
$$\heartsuit \text{Q}54$$

West, whose partner has bid hearts, starts with ♡6 against a no-trump contract. Declarer should play the king from dummy. If East ducks, declarer will score both the king and the queen; if instead East captures, he cannot safely continue the suit.

4

Playing the Right Card as Declarer

There are many situations where declarer can introduce an element
of doubt in a defender's mind. Suppose you are sitting South in a
major-suit game and West leads the ace of clubs, the suit lying like
this:

```
                ♣ 975
   ♣ AK103                 ♣ J84
                ♣ Q62
```

East plays the 4, his lowest card, to discourage a club continuation. If you follow with the 2, West can easily read the 4 as East's
lowest card; there will be no chance of the continuation for which
you are hoping. Suppose instead you play the 6. Now West may
continue the suit, placing his partner with Q 4 2 or perhaps 4 2. At
any rate an element of doubt is created.

Look at the opposite situation, where a continuation would be
unwelcome.

```
                ◇ 965
   ◇ AK104                 ◇ Q73
                ◇ J82
```

West starts with the ace and East signals encouragement with the
7. Playing the 8 from the South hand would not be a clever move; it
would make it all the clearer to West that East's 7 was an encouraging card. You should play the 2, leaving open the possibility that
East has J 8 7.

There is an easy way to remember the right action on these
occasions. Play *high* to encourage a continuation, *low* to discourage
– just as you would when defending.

Sometimes there is no easy rule to apply.

$\heartsuit$ Q97

$\heartsuit$ 2 $\heartsuit$ AK10654

$\heartsuit$ J83

You are playing in a suit contract after East has overcalled in hearts. West leads $\heartsuit$2, which you can read as a singleton, and East wins with the king. Which card should you play to deter a continuation?

Some players will have the jack on the table in quick time, feigning a singleton. This is a poor idea since most defenders do not lead the 2 from a holding such as 8 3 2 in partner's suit. The 8 (or the 3) is better, since it leaves open the possibility that West has led from J x x.

Bearing in mind the general idea of creating doubt in the defender's mind, try this situation.

$\spadesuit$ K875

$\spadesuit$ 2 $\spadesuit$ A9643

$\spadesuit$ QJ10

Against a suit contract West leads $\spadesuit$2 to his partner's ace. Do you have a card ready?

The jack is the only card to create any doubt. Most West players would have led the 2 from Q 10 2, but high from Q J 2 or J 10 2.

Even when a particular bluff is well known, there may still be doubt in the defender's mind.

$\clubsuit$ J74

$\clubsuit$ 6 $\clubsuit$ AQ109852

$\clubsuit$ K3

After East has opened three clubs West leads $\clubsuit$6 against a suit contract. South drops the king under the ace, a manoeuvre well publicised in bridge literature. It doesn't help East much to know that the king might be a false card; it might equally well be a singleton.

Occasionally the card you choose from dummy can have good effect.

$\diamondsuit$ KJ63

$\diamondsuit$ 5 $\diamondsuit$ A984

$\diamondsuit$ Q1072

Again West leads a singleton against a suit contract. Try the jack from dummy, dropping the 2 from hand. This will create the illusion that West has led from Q 10 7 5; East may switch his attack elsewhere.

Constant effort to play the right spot-card makes a difference on a surprising number of hands. The next deal is from a team-of-four match.

♠ AK5
♡ 973
$\diamondsuit$ J10963
♣ A4

♠ Q1063   ♠ J84
♡ QJ4   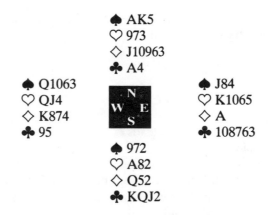   ♡ K1065
$\diamondsuit$ K874 $\diamondsuit$ A
♣ 95   ♣ 108763

♠ 972
♡ A82
$\diamondsuit$ Q52
♣ KQJ2

West led ♠3 against 3NT, dummy's ace winning the trick. A diamond went to East's ace and all depended on East's next move.

At one table East switched to a heart, breaking the contract (it does declarer no good to hold off ♡A twice, the defenders will switch back to spades). At the other table East persisted with spades and the contract was made.

When scores were compared the declarer who had gone down was none too pleased. 'A heart switch was obvious,' he complained.

'It wasn't that easy for me,' replied his team-mate. 'Declarer played the 7 at trick one, so I thought the lead was from a 5-card suit. You did the same, I suppose?'

It is often possible to interfere with the defenders' length signals.

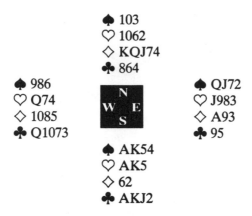

South plays in 3NT and is off to a good start when a club lead goes to the 9 and jack. It still seems that he will need two diamond tricks, though.

Suppose he leads ◇2 towards the king. West will play the 5, his lowest card, to show an odd number of cards in the suit (see Chapter 7). East, knowing now that South has only two diamonds (or four, in which case nothing can be done), will duck the first round of diamonds and win the second. One down.

A better prospect is for South to lead ◇6 to the king and continue with the queen. Now there is doubt in the defender's mind; perhaps West's 5 is from 5 2 and declarer has three diamonds. If East decides to play safe by holding off a second time declarer will have nine tricks.

In no-trump contracts it is often productive to disguise your strength in the suit led. You hope that the defenders will continue their attack in this quarter rather than switch to some unprotected flank.

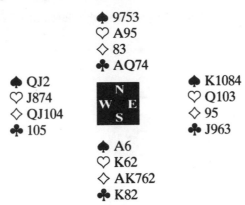

West leads the diamond queen against your 3NT, East playing the 5. Suppose you win and return a diamond, playing to establish a long card in that suit. A switch to spades will now put you down. A better idea is to duck the first round of diamonds, hoping for a diamond continuation which will give you a tempo. Which spot-card would you choose at trick one, to encourage a continuation?

The best card is the 6. If you play the 7 a suspicious West might ask himself where the 6 was. Expecting his partner to echo with the 6 from such as K 6 5 2, West might conclude that you were up to some sort of mischief.

Another camouflage technique is to win a trick with a higher card than is necessary. Imagination was needed to make the following contract.

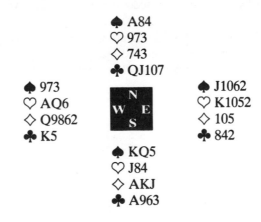

West led ◇6 against 3NT, East playing the 10. Declarer saw that all would be well if the club finesse was right. If this finesse lost, though, West might well switch to hearts. It was the right moment to feign weakness in the diamonds, encouraging the defenders to continue their attack in that quarter.

South won the first trick with the *king*, giving West the impression that his partner held the diamond jack. He then crossed to the ace of spades and ran the club queen. West won with the king and returned a diamond in quick time. The ninth trick, which declarer had temporarily surrendered at trick one, returned to the fold.

Another worthwhile technique is to disguise your strength in a suit you are establishing. Suppose that among your assets in a 3NT contract you have this club combination:

♣ 97642

♣ Q103   ♣ J5

♣ AK8

If you tackle the suit by playing ace, king and another, you may lose in two ways. First, the defenders will see that the suit is already established; they may realise the need to switch elsewhere for quick tricks. Secondly, East will have a chance to make an informative discard on the third round of clubs.

So, provided there is no problem with entries, it may be better to broach the suit by leading the 8 from hand, or possibly the ace followed by the 8. The principle, as always, is to create doubt in the mind of the defenders.

Even in the simplest of finessing positions there can be a right and a wrong card to play. Look at this common situation:

◇ K107

◇ A963   ◇ Q842

◇ J5

You are in a slam and everything depends on guessing this suit correctly. If you lead the jack it will be clear to West that you have a guess to make; he is likely to play low. If instead you lead the 5, West may fear that you have a singleton, perhaps with an unavoidable loser elsewhere. At any rate there is slightly more chance that he will give away the position by rising with the ace.

♣ 8532

♣ A6   ♣ J97

♣ KQ104

Suppose, in a no-trump contract, you start this suit with a low card to the king. West will expect you to hold the queen too; he may hold off the ace to present you with a guess on the next round. What will West's reaction be if instead you start with a low club to the queen? Now he may fear that you have Q J x x x and that a duck would lead to an embarrassing crash of honours on the next round. If he does decide to take his ace the odds will favour a finesse of the 10 on the next round.

5

First Off the Blocks

The choice of opening lead determines the fate of contract after contract. There is perhaps no area of the game where good players have a bigger advantage over average players.

To begin with, forget those tables of 'preferred leads' which have a smug A K Q at the top and a villainous K J x at the bottom; the lead is a tactical problem. We assume that you are familiar with the normal conventions concerning the choice of card from specific holdings and will therefore proceed directly to tactical considerations, first when leading against no-trumps.

The lead against no-trumps

The general rule, as of course you know, is to lead fourth best from your longest and strongest suit, or the highest of touching honours from combinations such as K Q J x x, K Q 10 x x or Q J 9 x x. From an interior sequence you lead the middle honour – the jack from K J 10 x x, the 10 from Q 10 9 x x.

This instruction will not take you far, though. For one thing, the object is not so much to lead from your own longest and strongest as to lead the longest and strongest held by the *partnership*. Let's look at a few examples where the bidding against you has been an uninformative 1NT–3NT.

(1)	♠ K108	(2)	♠ KJ85
	♡ 643		♡ 874
	◇ Q9752		◇ Q3
	♣ K4		♣ K1042

On (1) you would probably choose ◇5, because you have two potential entries to help you establish and enjoy the diamond suit. The lead might turn out poorly, but so might anything else. Suppose the hand were weaker – without ♣K; even then, the diamond would be a fair choice. Make the diamonds weaker, too – J x x x x – and the pendulum would swing; you would lead a heart, hoping to hit partner's length.

On (2) you have no five-card suit, so the choice is more delicate. The ♡8 might turn out well, but don't pay too much attention to the fact that a lead of a spade or a club is more likely to give up a trick. To beat the contract, you have to find five tricks from somewhere. As between a spade and a club, it is reasonable to take into account that the responder has not employed Stayman and is therefore not so likely to hold four spades himself. The ♠5 is narrowly best.

Suppose for a moment that the contract were 2NT, not 3NT, or even that the bidding had been 1NT–2NT–3NT. In each case there would be a presumption that the contract was going to be borderline. This makes a difference. It would be reasonable now to play a neutral game, leading ♡8 and letting the declarer find his own tricks.

(3)	♠ A762	(4)	♠ 632
	♡ K842		♡ A8
	◇ J953		◇ 10654
	♣ 6		♣ 9763

On (3) you have an awkward choice when leading against 3NT. A heart is slightly better than a spade, since the spade ace may act as a quick entry to enjoy a long heart. However, the ◇9 may well be a valuable card and most players would choose a diamond lead for that reason.

On (4) an important point is whether your partner has had a chance to show spades during the auction, either by opening or overcalling. If he spurned such an opportunity, a spade is unlikely to be productive and ◇4 is fractionally better than a club. (Concerning a club, most players nowadays lead second best from a four-card or longer suit containing no high honour.) If the opponents' auction gave partner no chance to speak, you must be more dynamic; the ♠6 would be a likely choice.

What of occasions when partner has bid a suit? There are various considerations.

(a) An opening bid of 1♣ or 1♢ by partner will often be based on a short suit (particularly if you play a strong no-trump), so you should have no hesitation in preferring a good lead of your own.

(b) If partner has overcalled, you need a pretty strong reason not to lead his suit. Very possibly he has taken a risk in overcalling; you will get the blame if instead of leading a singleton in his suit you set off on some wild excursion of your own. Any alternative, in general, should be at least as good as Q J 10 x x, with a sure side entry.

(c) The circumstances in which the opponents have gone to game in no-trumps over a bid by your side must be taken into consideration. If the declarer has bid no-trumps on the second or third round, then quite likely he has only a single stopper. It is a little different if he has propelled himself into 2NT or 3NT at his first opportunity.

One point we have not mentioned in this discussion is that partners who overcall on bad suits such as A J x x or K x x x x, thinking it clever to 'put in a bid', are a menace. Tell them so!

The lead against a suit contract

This is a difficult subject and the most profitable course may be to summarise the merits, or demerits, of the different types of lead.

Short suit leads

A singleton is usually a fair choice, the more so when you have the prospect of a trick in the trump suit. (In this case you may be able to find partner's entry on your second attempt.) Doubleton leads are overrated; they don't often lead to a ruff, and may assist declarer in setting up a side suit before you can reach your tricks elsewhere.

Lead from an honour combination

It is safer to lead from an honour that is supported (for example, K J x x or Q 10 x x) than from such as K x x x or Q x x x. Nevertheless, you will often have to lead from such moderate holdings in a suit that has not been mentioned.

Suppose the bidding has been:

South	North
1♠	2♣
2♠	4♠

. . . and you have to lead from one of these hands:

(5)		(6)	
	♠ 954		♠ 82
	♡ A62		♡ KJ74
	◇ K1075		◇ 10752
	♣ J93		♣ K85

Dummy is likely to hold a fair club suit and you can predict declarer's line of play; he will probably draw trumps and establish dummy's club suit. It is vital to attack in the red suits before he can do this. You should lead ◇5 on hand (1) and ♡4 on (2). Players who mumble 'when in doubt lead a trump' after an auction like this are not destined for stardom at the game.

Which card from three small?

What should you lead from a holding such as 8 5 3 in a suit that has not been mentioned? For decades it was standard to lead the top card, which at least had the merit of informing partner that you held no honour in the suit. The disadvantage was that partner could not tell on the first round, or quite possibly on the second round, whether you had led from two or three cards.

Many players sought an answer to this with what are called MUD leads, middle–up–down (in this case the 5 on the first round, the 8 on the second). A snag with this method is that by the time partner, with A K x x, has cashed the second winner, the damage may have been done.

In the USA there is support for a third method, leading low from x x x. The disadvantage of this is that partner sometimes cannot tell whether you are leading from strength or from weakness.

At present most tournament players lead the middle card; this is an area where you must discover what your partner expects.

Trump leads

There are two basic reasons why you may lead a trump. First, for safety when other leads are too likely to give away a trick. Second, when the auction suggests you may be able to cut down the ruffing potential of the dummy. The lead will seldom matter when there are four or more trumps in the dummy, but it may be important when the auction has been along these lines:

(A)	*South*	*North*	(B)	*South*	*North*
	1♠	1NT		1♠	1NT
	2♡	Pass		3♡	3NT
				4♡	Pass

In auction (A) North has given preference to partner's second suit; it is therefore quite possible that he has something like one spade and three hearts. A trump lead may well be good.

Auction (B) is similar. North will be very short in spades and you can expect declarer to try for some spade ruffs; consider a trump lead to thwart him.

If you decide that a trump lead is indicated, don't be dissuaded by a holding such as Q x x; usually the trick (if temporarily surrendered) will come back. Sometimes you will find partner with K x or A x and do declarer a considerable amount of damage.

It is important to distinguish between occasions when you, the opening leader, are strong in declarer's second suit and occasions when you expect partner to be strong in that department. Suppose the bidding goes:

South	North
1♠	1NT
3♡	3♠
4♠	Pass

. . . and you hold one of these hands:

(7)	♠ 74	(8)	♠ A84
	♡ KJ85		♡ 95
	◇ 10764		◇ Q863
	♣ K64		♣ K974

Many who write on the game will counsel a trump lead on (7). Really, this is not necessary because partner will no doubt be short in hearts and will probably be able to overruff the dummy and return a trump – a very effective defence. It is better to begin with a low club.

On (8), however, the danger of successful heart ruffs is strong. Ace and another spade may well be the game. At any rate, remember that it is when you are *short* in declarer's second suit that a trump lead is likely to be the best defence.

One final point. As a rule, avoid the lead of a singleton trump. This is because it may kill partner's Q x x or J 10 x x in the suit.

Forcing leads

The time for a forcing lead, designed to weaken the declarer's trump control, is normally when you hold four trumps yourself and a fairly long side suit.

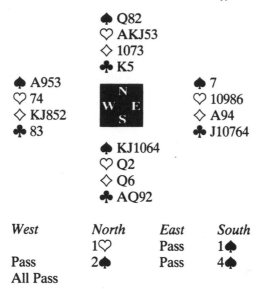

	♠ Q82		
	♡ AKJ53		
	◇ 1073		
	♣ K5		

♠ A953   ♠ 7
♡ 74   ♡ 10986
◇ KJ852   ◇ A94
♣ 83   ♣ J10764

♠ KJ1064
♡ Q2
◇ Q6
♣ AQ92

West	North	East	South
	1♡	Pass	1♠
Pass	2♣	Pass	4♠
All Pass			

West leads a diamond, commencing a forcing defence. The defenders persist with diamonds and South has to ruff the third round, reducing himself to four trumps. When declarer starts on the trumps West must duck the first two rounds, otherwise any further diamond force can be dealt with in the dummy. After this start declarer is helpless; he cannot prevent West scoring a second trump trick.

Most players appreciate the value of a forcing lead when they hold four trumps themselves. It's just as important to consider such a lead when you are short in trumps yourself and can expect partner to hold length.

Safe leads

Sometimes there is nothing to suggest a lead for any positive purpose, and the most you hope to do is to avoid giving a trick away. In this case a long suit, even such as J x x x x, is better than a four-card suit such as J x x x or 10 x x x. The longer the suit, the less likely that it will give away a trick.

Leading against slams

Against slams in no-trumps you should normally seek a passive lead.
A lead from such as K 10 x x x or Q 10 x x x may be fine against 3NT;
the prospect of establishing the long cards outweighs the risk of
giving away a trick initially. Against 6NT such a lead would be poor,
all too likely to concede a vital trick.

The situation is different against a small slam in a suit. Here
declarer will usually have the power to develop twelve tricks, given
the time. You may need to strike quickly to claim the tricks that are
yours.

Suppose the bidding has been in this confident fashion:

South	North
1♠	3♣
3♠	4NT
5♡	6♠
Pass	

. . . and you hold one of these hands:

(9)		(10)	
♠	63	♠	Q72
♡	K952	♡	854
◇	10654	◇	Q1085
♣	J83	♣	932

Go for gold! Lead ♡2 on hand (9), hoping to find partner with
♡A, or perhaps ♡Q and a quick trick elsewhere. From hand (10)
lead ◇5. You have hopes of a trump trick and the best chance of a
second trick lies in diamonds. On the occasions where this type of
attacking lead seems at first to give away a trick you will usually find
that the slam was cold anyway.

Against a grand slam in a suit the old-timers' advice was 'lead a
trump'. Certainly it is right to seek a passive lead (there can be no
advantage in establishing a trick against a grand!), and the assump-
tion was that a trump lead was certain to be safe. Nowadays, though,
plenty of grands are bid with a small hole in the trump suit, so as a
rule be reluctant to lead a *singleton* trump.

Summing up

You see, therefore, that the nature of the bidding is a better guide to the opening lead than the character of the suits held. You must *listen*. The type of player who asks 'Now, what's the contract?' or 'My lead, is it?' is unlikely to be a dynamo at the game.

6

Planning the Defence

Your partner makes the opening lead and the dummy goes down. The declarer, if he is sensible, pauses awhile before playing a card from dummy, however obvious this card may be. He is forming a plan, and he is taking advantage of the fact that, seeing two hands in partnership, he has at this stage a decided advantage over the defenders. Finally he plays a card from dummy and perhaps in third position you play the obvious card from your own hand, a card that requires no thought.

Have you been resting meanwhile? If so, that is wrong – badly wrong. Whether the declarer plays quickly or slowly from dummy at trick one, you have every right to reflect on the situation. Ask yourself questions such as the following:

Thinking back to the bidding, is the dummy weaker or stronger than it might have been? How do your high cards sit in relation to those in the dummy? These matters will at least enable you to ponder on your chances of success. Will the contract be a 'damned close-run thing', as somebody once said about the Battle of Waterloo, or will heroic measures be needed to give your side a chance?

Again, looking at your hand and the dummy's, and remembering the bidding, how much can you infer about declarer's holding? What evidence is there as to his 'points' and distribution?

Next, what conclusions can you draw from partner's lead? Why has he chosen this particular suit? What does it tell you about his holding in the other suits? Suppose partner does not lead the suit you have called. Why not? In a trump contract he may have too many to make it worthwhile attacking this suit. If it is no-trumps he may have such as Ax, sitting over declarer's likely queen or king.

By the time you have thought about questions of this kind you will be far more capable of planning a good defence than if you simply play a card and wait to see what happens later.

Defending in the second seat

The basic rule here is 'second hand plays low'. It's easy to see why by looking at a few situations where inexperienced players go wrong.

♠ Q54

♠ K963   ♠ A102

♠ J87

South leads the 7 towards dummy. If West plays his king on thin air declarer's queen and jack will produce a trick.

♡ J75

♡ Q92   ♡ K863

♡ A104

Declarer leads the 4. If West is tempted to rise with the queen it will cost his side a trick.

Sometimes playing high will save declarer a guess in the suit. Suppose you are West here:

♢ Q954

♢ K63   ♢ J87

♢ A102

If declarer leads low from hand, at least give him the chance to finesse dummy's 9.

It often happens that declarer leads a side-suit singleton from dummy. What is your reaction, sitting in the next seat, when you hold the ace? You play it? More often than not, this is wrong. This deal is typical.

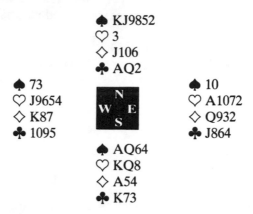

♠ KJ9852
♡ 3
♢ J106
♣ AQ2

♠ 73
♡ J9654
♢ K87
♣ 1095

♠ 10
♡ A1072
♢ Q932
♣ J864

♠ AQ64
♡ KQ8
♢ A54
♣ K73

South plays in six spades and your partner leads a club, won by the king. Declarer draws two rounds of trumps and follows with dummy's singleton heart. What will happen if you take your ace? It will be the last trick for your side; declarer will discard two of dummy's diamonds on ♡KQ. Hold off the ace and you will lose one trick in hearts, gain two in diamonds.

Another reason to play low in this situation is that declarer may have a guess in the suit.

♠ 3

♠ Q104

♠ A9762

♠ KJ85

Here it would be feeble to go in with the ace, however many discards are needed.

Rules are made to be broken and 'second hand low' is no exception. There are a few specific situations where the second player needs to rise with an honour. This is a common one:

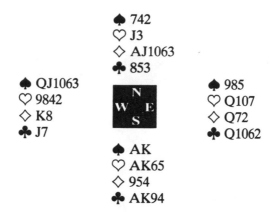

```
                ♠ 742
                ♡ J3
                ♢ AJ1063
                ♣ 853
♠ QJ1063                      ♠ 985
♡ 9842          N             ♡ Q107
♢ K8        W       E         ♢ Q72
♣ J7            S             ♣ Q1062
                ♠ AK
                ♡ AK65
                ♢ 954
                ♣ AK94
```

Against 3NT West starts with the spade queen, won by declarer's king. A low diamond is led. See what happens if West plays low to this trick. The 10 is played from dummy and whether or not East wins with the queen declarer will score four diamond tricks, making an easy overtrick.

West can interrupt the flow of the diamond suit by rising with the king on the first round. If declarer captures with the ace East will duck the next round, restricting declarer to two tricks in the suit. Declarer will do no better to allow West's king to win; the defenders will then clear the spade suit.

Another good time to play high in second position is when you need to conserve partner's entry in that suit. This usually happens at no-trumps.

♠ AQ7
♡ 92
◇ J10963
♣ 853

♠ 1062   ♠ 9853
♡ KJ874   N   ♡ 1063
◇ K8   W   E ◇ A4
♣ Q74   S   ♣ J1062

♠ KJ4
♡ AQ5
◇ Q752
♣ AK9

Partner leads ♡7 against South's 3NT contract, drawing the 9, 10 and queen. Declarer now crosses to dummy with a spade and leads the jack of diamonds. If you play low you have missed the only chance of beating the contract. Your partner can win with the king but declarer will now duck the second round of hearts. When you win the second round of diamonds you will have no heart left.

See how easily the defence runs if you rise with the ace of diamonds. You clear the heart suit and partner still has the king of diamonds as an entry. The same play would be right if you held the king of diamonds and partner the ace.

Defending in the third seat

Here the general rule is 'third hand plays high'. With two high cards of equal rank you play the *lower* card; has it ever struck you why?

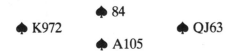

♠ 84

♠ K972   ♠ QJ63

♠ A105

The 2 is led and East's jack forces the ace. West can deduce that East has the queen, since otherwise declarer would presumably have won with this card. A similar inference would not be available if East were to play high from touching cards; declarer might well hold the jack in that case.

The situation is not quite so easy when there is a high card in the dummy.

$$\heartsuit \; Q65$$

$\heartsuit$ KJ84 $\heartsuit$ A103

$$\heartsuit \; 972$$

West starts with the 4 and declarer plays low from dummy. Now East must play the 10, keeping the ace as a policeman to dummy's queen. If East plays the ace at trick 1 the queen will eventually score a trick.

Playing the 10 in this position will allow declarer to score the jack if he has it. In a no-trump contract this would not matter too much, since declarer would score a trick in the suit anyway. In a suit contract, where it might be disastrous to let declarer win the first trick from J x, East would have to consider playing the ace. Indeed, this would probably be right, because partner is more likely to have led from K x x x than from J x x x.

$$\clubsuit \; K104$$

$\clubsuit$ Q962 $\clubsuit$ J83

$$\clubsuit \; A75$$

This position is similar; you should play the 8, keeping the jack to deal with dummy's 10. In these examples you are finessing against the dummy, not committing the traditional gaffe of finessing against partner.

Sometimes the right play in the third seat may seem to be something of a guess.

$$\diamondsuit \; Q6$$

$\diamondsuit$ A8753 $\diamondsuit$ K1042

$$\diamondsuit \; J9$$

West leads $\diamondsuit$5 against a no-trump contract and dummy plays low. If West has led from the jack and declarer has the ace, East's best play is the 10. If the cards lie as in the diagram, he does best to rise with the king. How can East know what to do?

The answer is that declarer can hardly hold A x or A x x, or he would surely have risen with dummy's queen. East should therefore play the king at trick 1.

When to cover an honour

You will have heard the saying 'always cover an honour with an honour'. In truth, decisions on whether or not to cover are often far more complex than some bridge books admit. Let's see first the basic purpose of covering.

$$\spadesuit \text{ AQ105}$$

$$\spadesuit \text{ K83} \qquad\qquad \spadesuit \text{ 9642}$$

$$\spadesuit \text{ J7}$$

It's a familiar situation: West must cover the jack or declarer will end with four tricks.

There are many situations, though, where it can cost a trick to cover.

$$\heartsuit \text{ QJ82}$$

$$\heartsuit \text{ 1075} \qquad\qquad \heartsuit \text{ K63}$$

$$\heartsuit \text{ A94}$$

If East covers the queen declarer will win with the ace and run the 9 on the next round, scoring four tricks in the suit. East should let the queen pass, holding declarer to three tricks. In general, do not cover honour cards which are touching.

$$\clubsuit \text{ A64}$$

$$\clubsuit \text{ K83} \qquad\qquad \clubsuit \text{ 1075}$$

$$\clubsuit \text{ QJ92}$$

Here is the same situation from the other side. Again, when the queen is led, West should not cover. (If South, either a genius or a novice, has led the queen from Q x x, give him the money this time.)

◇ A72

◇ K94 ◇ Q853

◇ J106

Similarly, it will be expensive if West covers the jack here. Declarer will win and lead back towards the 10, scoring an undeserved second trick.

Sometimes the correct play is unclear.

♠ AJ63

♠ Q72 ♠ 84

♠ K1095

When South advances the 10 West may put on the queen. 'Well, it was awkward for me,' he will say, when this saves declarer a guess in the suit. 'Declarer might have held 10 x x.'

The point here is that with K 10 9 x declarer will always try this ruse. With 10 x x he has other approaches open to him; normally he will lead low to the jack, a play that will fare well when West has a doubleton honour. It follows that when the 10 is led West should not cover, nor show any sign of thinking about it.

Always keep in mind that the object of covering an honour is to promote a subsequent trick for your side. You don't want to look foolish by covering in a situation of this kind:

♡ J863

♡ A ♡ K5

♡ Q109742

This is the trump suit and wily South leads the jack from dummy. There will surely have been indications in the bidding that declarer holds length, not just A Q x x (in which case he would have led a low card from dummy, anyway). So, it is pointless to cover; you cannot promote any holding in partner's hand. A cover will prove disastrous in the position shown, also if your partner has a singleton queen. Another good reason to cherish the king is that there are plenty of declarers who, holding A Q 10 x x x, will then play for the drop.

This is another position of the same kind:

                 ♣ 1074

♣ Q   ♣ J93

                 ♣ AK8652

If the bidding leads him to think West is short of the suit, declarer may think of leading the 10 from dummy. If East is unwise enough to cover, the ace and queen will complete the trick and declarer will finesse the 8 on the next round. (If West was so brilliant as to play the queen from Q 9 doubleton . . . buy him a drink.)

Deductions from declarer's play

Conclusions can often be drawn from declarer's early play. Let's look at a few familiar situations:

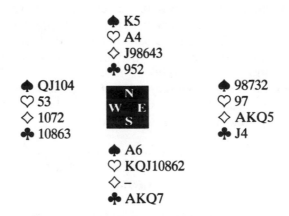

                   ♠ K5
                   ♡ A4
                   ♢ J98643
                   ♣ 952

♠ QJ104   ♠ 98732
♡ 53   ♡ 97
♢ 1072   ♢ AKQ5
♣ 10863   ♣ J4

                   ♠ A6
                     ♡ KQJ10862
                   ♢ –
                   ♣ AKQ7

South arrives in seven hearts and wins the spade lead with dummy's king. He now runs the trump suit. On the last trump West has to find a discard from ♠J10 ♣10863. What should he throw?

There are more ways than one for West to know what he should do. For example, East could discard several spades 'upwards', making it clear to West that declarer has no spade threat. Still, that is hardly necessary in the present case; it's pretty obvious, really, that if declarer had held a third spade *he would have ruffed it in dummy before drawing trumps!*

Even declarers who are not all that clever usually have some reason for their early play. Always try to discern what your opponent has in mind.

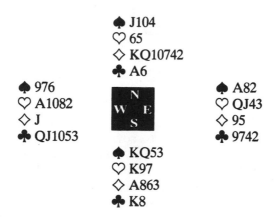

```
                    ♠ J104
                    ♡ 65
                    ◇ KQ10742
                    ♣ A6
    ♠ 976                          ♠ A82
    ♡ A1082       N                ♡ QJ43
    ◇ J        W     E             ◇ 95
    ♣ QJ1053      S                ♣ 9742
                    ♠ KQ53
                    ♡ K97
                    ◇ A863
                    ♣ K8
```

South opens 1NT and is raised to 3NT. West leads the club queen, won by the ace, and declarer, trying to look like a man who is about to finesse, leads the jack of spades from dummy. Sitting East, what should you do?

The first inference is that since declarer has not played on diamonds that suit is ready to run. You know that declarer has the top two clubs, bringing his total to eight, so if the contract is to be beaten he cannot hold the ace of hearts too. So, rise with the ace of spades and switch to the heart queen.

It frequently happens in a no-trump contract that declarer holds up twice in the suit led and you place him with A x x. Don't automatically play a third round. He may have been forced to hold up because of the danger in this particular suit; he may also be open to attack in another quarter. For example:

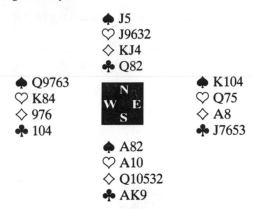

♠ J5
♡ J9632
◇ KJ4
♣ Q82

♠ Q9763
♡ K84
◇ 976
♣ 104

♠ K104
♡ Q75
◇ A8
♣ J7653

♠ A82
♡ A10
◇ Q10532
♣ AK9

Against 3NT West leads ♠6, covered by the jack and king. Declarer holds off and allows East's ♠10 to win the next trick, noting meanwhile that West (by leading the 6 and following with the 3) has indicated a five-card suit. At this stage a number of defenders would clear the spades. This would not be good enough on the present hand, since declarer has nine tricks once the diamond ace has been removed.

Instead, East, knowing that he will come in with the ace of diamonds, should seek two tricks in hearts, leading low to his partner's king. East plays low on the second round of hearts and the heart queen becomes the setting trick. You may think that a spade continuation would work better if West had the ace of hearts, and declarer perhaps K 10 x. If that were the situation, though, partner would surely have overtaken the second spade and cleared the suit himself.

All the time ask yourself 'What's declarer going to try? Can I intervene in time?' East had to move at top speed on this deal:

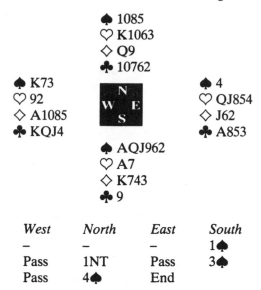

♠ 1085
♡ K1063
◇ Q9
♣ 10762

♠ K73
♡ 92
◇ A1085
♣ KQJ4

♠ 4
♡ QJ854
◇ J62
♣ A853

♠ AQJ962
♡ A7
◇ K743
♣ 9

West	North	East	South
–	–	–	1♠
Pass	1NT	Pass	3♠
Pass	4♠	End	

West led ♣K and East turned his mind to declarer's likely line of play. Hearts were tied up and South was likely to be short in clubs; he might well need to score one or more diamond ruffs in dummy.

East overtook his partner's club lead with the ace and fired back his singleton trump. This fine defence put the contract two down; declarer had to lose three diamond tricks. Anything less dynamic from East and ten tricks would be there.

7

Putting Partner in the Picture

Declarer can see his combined assets right from the opening gun. The defenders are not so fortunate and can let each other know what they hold only by passing signals. There are three basic types of signal. When doubt exists, this is the order of preference:

(1) **Attitude:** on the opening lead, especially, you play a high card when you wish to encourage, your lowest card when enthusiasm is absent.

(2) **Distribution:** The signal to express an odd or even number of cards in the suit (low for odd, high for even) occurs mainly when the opponent has led a suit. Even on partner's leads, though, there are occasions when 'attitude' is plainly of no importance – a distributional signal may then be given.

(3) **Suit preference:** When the situation is such that neither 'attitude' nor 'distribution' could be of interest, an unnecessarily high card may indicate values in the higher of the alternative suits, a low card values in the lower suit. This technique is common in tournament play, less so at rubber bridge.

Attitude signals on partner's lead

Suppose your partner (West) leads the king of clubs, either at trick 1 or in the middle of the play, and the suit lies like this:

♣ 976

♣ KQ104   ♣ 853

♣ AJ2

You signal with the 3 – an attitude signal, discouraging a continuation of the suit. If South ducks, West will not be tempted to play a second round.

A low signal does not necessarily deny a high card in the suit but it does suggest that partner might do better to look elsewhere. This deal is an example:

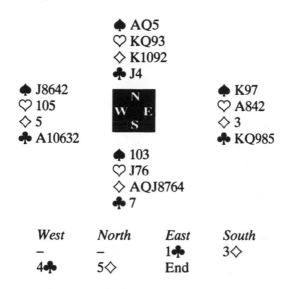

♠ AQ5
♡ KQ93
◇ K1092
♣ J4

♠ J8642   ♠ K97
♡ 105   ♡ A842
◇ 5   ◇ 3
♣ A10632   ♣ KQ985

♠ 103
♡ J76
◇ AQJ8764
♣ 7

West	North	East	South
–	–	1♣	3◇
4♣	5◇	End	

West leads ♣A and East sees that a spade switch is likely to beat the contract. Despite holding ♣KQ, therefore, he discourages with the 5. A heart switch could serve little purpose, so West plays a spade at trick 2, establishing a third trick for the defence. (A surprising *queen* of clubs from East would convey the same message – lead a spade.)

Signalling with an honour

When you signal with an honour you indicate at least one touching honour below the card you throw; you deny the honour directly above.

$$\diamondsuit \text{ A85}$$
$$\diamondsuit \text{ 92} \qquad\qquad \diamondsuit \text{ QJ1043}$$
$$\diamondsuit \text{ K76}$$

West leads $\diamondsuit$9 and declarer plays the ace from dummy. If East chooses to signal with the queen he will deny the king but promise the jack (and presumably, in this case, the 10).

This is a common situation:

$$\heartsuit \text{ 105}$$
$$\heartsuit \text{ AK872} \qquad\qquad \heartsuit \text{ QJ6}$$
$$\heartsuit \text{ 943}$$

Against a suit contract West leads the ace (or king, if this is his method) and East signals with the queen. It may now suit West to cross to his partner's jack on the next round. Since the queen has this particular meaning, East must not peter when he holds Qx in the suit led.

Showing distribution on partner's lead

Quite often there is no point in displaying 'attitude' and the defender may instead indicate his distribution in the suit led. This is usually when he cannot beat the card played by second hand.

$$\spadesuit \text{ QJ4}$$
$$\spadesuit \text{ K10852} \qquad\qquad \spadesuit \text{ 963}$$
$$\spadesuit \text{ A7}$$

West starts with $\spadesuit$5 against a no-trump contract and dummy's queen is played. East cannot beat the queen and sees that partner may well be interested in how many cards declarer holds in the suit. He therefore gives a distributional signal – the 3, indicating an odd number of cards in the suit. When West gains the lead he will know it is safe to continue with a low spade, clearing the suit. Had East started with just ♠93 he would play the 9, which in this case would warn West not to continue.

Often, in a suit contract, it may be clear that to show strength or weakness would be idle.

♣ J65

♣ KQ102   ♣ 9873

♣ A4

When West leads ♣K against a high suit contract the most important message that East can convey is that he has an even number. If West subsequently gains the lead he will know that a second club will stand up.

Suit preference signals

This type of signal is common in tournament play, not so much in the rubber game. Sometimes there is no point in either an attitude signal (the first priority) or a distributional signal (the second priority). In such cases only, a signal may be read as suit preference. This is such a case:

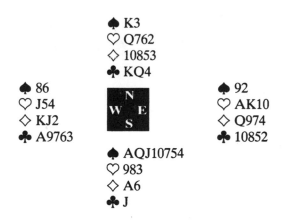

South opens four spades, passed out, and West makes the unfortunate start of the club ace. There can be no purpose in a (presumably discouraging!) attitude signal. Nor can West be vaguely interested in how many clubs East holds. East is then free to play the 10 of clubs – a high suit preference signal, indicating interest in the higher of the other two side suits. West duly switches to ♡J and the contract breathes its last.

The most common use of suit preference signals is when you are giving partner a ruff. The size of the card led will indicate which suit you would like him to return.

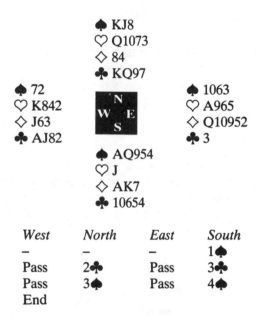

| ♠ KJ8 |
| ♡ Q1073 |
| ♢ 84 |
| ♣ KQ97 |

♠ 72   ♠ 1063
♡ K842   ♡ A965
♢ J63   ♢ Q10952
♣ AJ82   ♣ 3

| ♠ AQ954 |
| ♡ J |
| ♢ AK7 |
| ♣ 10654 |

West	North	East	South
–	–	–	1♠
Pass	2♣	Pass	3♣
Pass	3♠	Pass	4♠
End			

West, who can expect the opponents to hold at least eight clubs between them, makes the bright start of the ace of clubs. He now has a choice of clubs to lead at trick 2. Since his best chance of a re-entry is in hearts, the higher of the other two side suits, he follows with the jack of clubs. East ruffs and respects his partner's signal by returning a low heart. West wins with the king and can now deliver a second ruff to sink the contract.

Showing distribution on declarer's suits

We look next at the situation when declarer is playing on one of his own suits. Here the defenders' duty may be to show each other their distribution in the suit. There are many situations where this will aid the defence, particularly when a defender has to judge whether or not to hold up a high card.

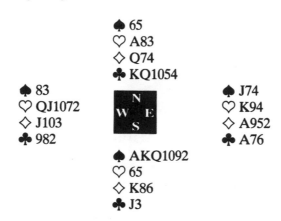

　　　　　♠ 65
　　　　　♡ A83
　　　　　♢ Q74
　　　　　♣ KQ1054

♠ 83　　　　　　　　　　　♠ J74
♡ QJ1072　　　　　　　　♡ K94
♢ J103　　　　　　　　　　♢ A952
♣ 982　　　　　　　　　　♣ A76

　　　　　♠ AKQ1092
　　　　　♡ 65
　　　　　♢ K86
　　　　　♣ J3

Against four spades West leads ♡Q, won in the dummy. Declarer draws trumps in three rounds, then plays a low club to the king. If East grabs this, hoping to cash three more tricks in the red suits, he will regret it; declarer can enter dummy in clubs to take one or more discards.

In this situation West must let his partner know how many clubs declarer holds by signalling his own length. Here West would play the 2, indicating an odd number of clubs. East should then hold off the first round of clubs. Subsequently he can win the second round of clubs and exit with king and another heart, leaving declarer to lose two diamond tricks.

Did you notice that declarer in fact misplayed the hand? After drawing trumps he should have played a second round of hearts. However the defenders play, declarer can ruff dummy's last heart when the first round of clubs is ducked; East will then have no happy return when he wins the second club.

Discarding

The traditional method of discarding is **attitude** – a high discard shows interest in that suit, a low card disinterest.

The first discard was of crucial importance on this deal from matchplay.

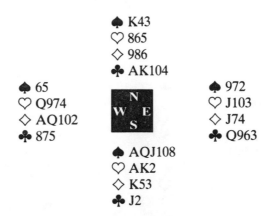

```
                    ♠ K43
                    ♡ 865
                    ◇ 986
                    ♣ AK104
    ♠ 65                          ♠ 972
    ♡ Q974          N            ♡ J103
    ◇ AQ102      W     E         ◇ J74
    ♣ 875           S            ♣ Q963
                    ♠ AQJ108
                    ♡ AK2
                    ◇ K53
                    ♣ J2
```

South played in four spades and West led a trump. Declarer continued to draw trumps and on the third round West discarded ♡4, indicating lack of interest in that suit. Declarer now ran ♣J, losing to East's queen. Bearing partner's signal in mind, East switched to diamonds, correctly playing the jack. The defenders snaffled three quick tricks in the suit to put the contract one down.

Declarer played the hand without guile. Suppose he plays a low club to the 10 at trick 2. East will now have to make his switch without the help of a discard from his partner. He is likely to prefer his J 10 combination and declarer will emerge alive. He will win the heart switch and draw two rounds of trumps with the ace and queen. He can then unblock ♣J and cross to dummy's king of trumps to take two discards.

8

Playing the Right Card as Defender

Some defenders – the majority, in fact – are 'easy'. They take their winners when offered, they false-card only in situations where they always false-card, and they rarely find the switch that will make life difficult for you. In this chapter we look at ways in which good defenders make life awkward for declarer, in particular at the opportunities for clever play within a single suit.

Playing the card you are known to hold

Imagine you are East here:

$$\clubsuit \text{ K974}$$

$$\clubsuit \text{ 865} \qquad\qquad \clubsuit \text{ Q103}$$

$$\clubsuit \text{ AJ2}$$

Declarer finesses the jack and continues with the ace on the second round. Sitting East, you must not follow with the 10 in supine fashion. If you do that, South will not need to be a world champion to collect four tricks from the suit. Instead, you must play the queen on the second round, because this is the card you are known to hold. South may then place your partner with 10–x–x–x and finesse the 9 on the next round. Even if he is familiar with the deception he will still be unsure what to do next.

The same kind of opportunity often occurs with a K–J combination. After declarer has successfully finessed the queen, the king and jack are equals and you must not fail to drop the king on the next round. This type of situation often arises in a suit contract:

$\diamondsuit$ AQ952

$\diamondsuit$ KJ84 $\diamondsuit$ 106

$\diamondsuit$ 73

Playing to establish tricks in a side suit before trumps have been drawn, South finesses the queen and follows with the ace. Drop the king now (do the same if you have begun with only K J x). Once you have done this, declarer cannot be sure whether it will be safe to ruff the next round with a low trump. He may abandon the suit or he may (if East follows to the third round) nervously ruff high.

Creating a losing option

Imaginative defence can sometimes create a losing option for declarer where none previously existed.

$\diamondsuit$ KQ95

$\diamondsuit$ J83 $\diamondsuit$ 1062

$\diamondsuit$ A74

If declarer starts this suit by playing ace and another, it costs West nothing to play the jack on the second round. Declarer may form the impression that West has split his honours from J 10 8 3, a play that might be necessary had declarer held only two diamonds. In that case he may return to the South hand to finesse the 9.

This is another situation where you can dangle some bait before declarer's nose:

$\heartsuit$ KJ62

$\heartsuit$ Q74 $\heartsuit$ 108

$\heartsuit$ A953

It's not very original but when the ace is led you may follow with the 10 in the East seat. An unsuspecting declarer may now play you for Q 10 doubleton.

Mind you, it doesn't pay to make a habit of this particular false card. If a wily declarer becomes aware of it he may catch you in this position:

$\heartsuit$ KJ62

$\heartsuit$ 1074 $\heartsuit$ Q8

$\heartsuit$ A953

Needing to pick up the suit, declarer starts with ace and another, West following with the 4 and the 7. A finesse of the jack will win only when East started with 10 8 doubleton. If East would *always* false-card from that holding declarer may elect to rise with dummy's king, dropping East's queen!

Many battles have been fought around this combination:

♣ AJ9

♣   ♣ K863

Q104

♣ 752

South's best chance of two tricks is to lead to the 9, gaining when West holds Q 10 or K 10; the alternative, leading to the jack, would gain only against K Q. Suppose West rises with the queen, though. Declarer may form the view that West has split his honours from K Q. Of course, if West *always* plays the honour from an honour–10 combination a different inference will be available when he plays low. Declarer may place him with the king and queen and finesse dummy's jack successfully! The best idea, as a defender, is to vary one's play in this type of situation.

There is a well-known swindle here:

♠ 96

♠ J73   ♠ AK852

♠ Q104

South plays in a no-trump contract after East has shown his spades. West leads the 3 and East wins deceptively with the ace, implying that he does not hold the king. When a low card is returned declarer may finesse the 10, hoping that East has A J x x x.

There are many similar positions where you can put declarer to a guess.

♣ 1064

♣ AJ3   ♣ Q982

♣ K75

If East is looking for tricks in this suit he should start with the queen. Declarer must now guess who holds the jack. If he reads East for Q J x and holds off the king the defenders will pocket three quick tricks.

This is a related position:

♢ 1072

♢ J95   ♢
                AQ64

♢ K83

Again East starts with the queen. If declarer ducks this, and plays low again on the next round, the defenders will have a good story to tell.

Here is another pretty play, not at all well known:

♢ J74

♢ Q102   ♢ K853

♢ A96

If you have to attack this suit from the East side, lead the king! South is sure to place you with the queen too and duck from hand. It's the same, of course, if East holds Q x x x and West K 10 x.

Obligatory false cards

There are a few situations where a false card is absolutely necessary to give declarer a guess.

♢ AQ862

♢ K5   ♢ 1094

♢ J73

Say that declarer finesses the queen and East plays the 4. Declarer has no option now but to play the ace on the next round, bringing in the suit. Instead East should drop the 9 or 10. Now declarer may decide to lead the jack on the next round, playing East for 10 9 doubleton.

$$\diamondsuit \text{ AJ9852}$$
$$\diamondsuit \text{ 1063} \qquad\qquad \diamondsuit \text{ KQ}$$
$$\diamondsuit \text{ 74}$$

Here declarer finesses dummy's 9, losing to the queen (or king). When a second round is led West *must* put in the 10, giving South the option of playing him for K 10 x (or Q 10 x). If West follows with an unthinking 6, declarer's only chance of bringing in the suit is to rise with the ace.

Take the West cards here:

$$\diamondsuit \text{ 63}$$
$$\diamondsuit \text{ J97} \qquad\qquad \diamondsuit \text{ A2}$$
$$\diamondsuit \text{ KQ10854}$$

Declarer starts with a low card to the king (or queen). If dummy is short of entries you may start by dropping the 9. Now South may be tempted to continue with the king, hoping that you have J 9 alone.

As a matter of fact, a great number of deceptions are playable with J 9, K J 9, A J 9, and some with Q 10 or 10 8. The great Italian player, Benito Garozzo, claims many successes with the king from K J. But no, we don't advise you to try that!

Playing the right card through

Leaving deception aside for the moment, there are many single-suit situations where a defender must lead the right card.

♡ 1065

♡ A43   ♡ KJ92

♡ Q87

Suppose East has to start this suit. Since his jack and 9 *surround* dummy's 10, he should lead the jack. South will lose three tricks, whether or not he covers the jack.

This is a similar position:

♠ 973

♠ K65   ♠ Q1082

♠ AJ4

If East leads a low card, declarer can score two tricks by playing low. Instead East should note that his 10 and 8 surround dummy's 9. Leading the 10 will hold declarer to one trick.

Preserving communications

On now to something different – preserving the line of communication with your partner. This is one position you will surely know:

◇ 97

◇ A10862   ◇ K53

◇ QJ4

Against a no-trump contract West leads the 5 to East's king and back comes the 5, covered by the queen. West must duck, of course.

The suit might instead lie like this, though:

$$\heartsuit\ 97$$

$$\heartsuit\ A10862 \qquad\qquad \heartsuit\ KJ53$$

$$\heartsuit\ Q4$$

Now a second-round duck from West might be disastrous. The solution is for East to return the *middle* card from a three-card holding, otherwise his original *fourth best*. Here East will return the 3, proclaiming either four or two hearts. West can see that a hold-up would be pointless.

There is one type of hand where East has to do something clever with his first card, rather than the second. Suppose you are East on this deal, defending 3NT.

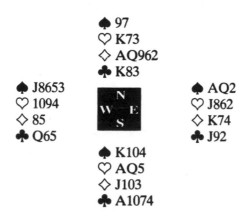

♠ 97
♥ K73
♦ AQ962
♣ K83

♠ J8653
♥ 1094
♦ 85
♣ Q65

♠ AQ2
♥ J862
♦ K74
♣ J92

♠ K104
♥ AQ5
♦ J103
♣ A1074

Partner leads ♠5 and let's say that you win with the ace. You return the spade queen, declarer holding off, and continue with your last spade, taken by the king. The diamond finesse loses but since you have no spade to return declarer scores an easy ten tricks. What could you have done about it?

Your aim should be to prevent declarer from holding up his spade stopper. Suppose you play the queen at trick 1. South can hardly hold off, because if West had led from A J x x x you would now run the whole suit. South is therefore likely to win the first trick, then take the diamond finesse. Now four spade tricks are yours.

The same type of play gains in other situations.

West leads ♠6 against 3NT. If, as East, you expect to gain the lead later, it will usually be right for you to play the jack now. This might cost a trick unnecessarily if declarer had only Q x x, but that will hardly matter if partner has five spades and the contract goes one down anyway.

9

Closing the Escape Route

Whenever you are blessed with plenty of trumps in both hands you should turn your mind towards what is known as 'elimination play'. The idea is simple. You eliminate from your own hand and dummy the suits that an opponent could play with safety; then you put him on lead, forcing him to open a suit to your advantage. The deal below is a standard example of what is called a ruff-and-discard elimination:

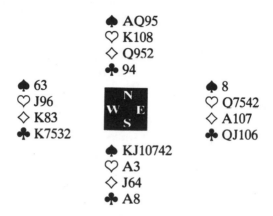

♠ AQ95
♡ K108
◇ Q952
♣ 94

♠ 63
♡ J96
◇ K83
♣ K7532

♠ 8
♡ Q7542
◇ A107
♣ QJ106

♠ KJ10742
♡ A3
◇ J64
♣ A8

West leads a trump against four spades. You draw a second round and can easily make a certainty of the contract. Don't play on diamonds, hoping for a favourable position there. Instead, cash the top hearts and ruff a heart, *eliminating* the hearts. Then play ace and another club, leaving one or other defender on lead. He will be forced to open the diamonds or concede a ruff-and-discard. If he chooses a diamond you will be in no danger of losing three tricks in the suit.

This hand would be slightly more tricky if you held AQ of clubs instead of Ax. If you finessed in clubs and diamonds you might go down. Instead, follow the same line as before: eliminate the hearts, then play ace and queen of clubs, disdaining the finesse.

The diamond situation in the hand we have just seen is one of a great number where you will be well placed after elimination. Here are some others.

(1)	AQ9	(2)	K104	(3)	QJ4
	762		853		762

With all these holdings you are safe to lose the minimum whether you lead the suit yourself or an opponent has to start it. You will lead to the 9 on (1), to the 10 on (2). It won't matter if East holds all the missing honours; when he wins the first trick he will be on play. On (3) you will survive even if East holds A K 10.

(4)	K62	(5)	Q62	(6)	A54
	J43		K107		J83

With (4) you are assured of a trick if your opponents are forced to play the suit. With (5) elimination will certainly improve your chances of making two tricks. If West has to lead the suit you are home already. If East leads, then you put in the 10 and at worst cover the jack with the queen. You may still find East with the ace, so you are roughly 3–1 on to make two tricks. A great many elimination plays are like this; they give you an extra chance, success not guaranteed.

On (6), with the opponents opening the suit, you hope that the king and queen lie together. If you have to open the suit yourself, you can play East for both the missing honours (starting with a low card towards the jack). The main point to note is that you can never be worse off if the opponents have to open a suit.

Now that you have the general idea, let's see how quickly you pick out the right line on these hands. On the first you are in six spades and West leads ♡Q.

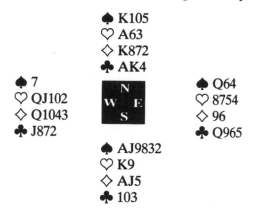

♠ K105
♥ A63
♦ K872
♣ AK4

♠ 7
♥ QJ102
♦ Q1043
♣ J872

♠ Q64
♥ 8754
♦ 96
♣ Q965

♠ AJ9832
♥ K9
♦ AJ5
♣ 103

There are possible losers in trumps and diamonds and you must try to arrange the play so that if you misguess in trumps the defenders may have to help you in diamonds. You win the heart lead in the South hand and cross to ♠K. Next you eliminate hearts and clubs, ruffing with the 9 and 8 to minimise the risk of an overruff. Finally you cross to ♦K and *finesse* the jack of trumps. If the finesse loses, West will have no good return; he will have to lead into your diamond tenace or concede a ruff-and-discard. As it happens, the trump finesse wins and you can look for an overtrick by taking the diamond finesse.

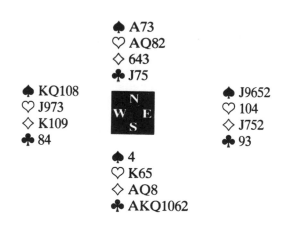

♠ A73
♥ AQ82
♦ 643
♣ J75

♠ KQ108
♥ J973
♦ K109
♣ 84

♠ J9652
♥ 104
♦ J752
♣ 93

♠ 4
♥ K65
♦ AQ8
♣ AKQ1062

You play in six clubs against a spade lead. If you simply play for a 3–3 break in hearts and then take the diamond finesse, you will fail.

You should win the spade lead, ruff a spade, draw trumps and ruff the last spade. Now take three rounds of hearts. They don't break, but as West holds the fourth heart you can throw him in, discarding ◇8 from hand. He will then have to lead into the diamond A Q or concede a ruff-and-discard. The play is called a loser-on-loser elimination.

A combination such as A x x opposite J x x x gives you elimination chances which may not at first be obvious. The defenders sometimes have an opportunity to shine too.

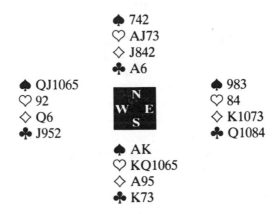

West leads ♠Q against six hearts. There is more than one way to play this contract. You could eliminate the black suits, then lead a low diamond towards the jack, playing West for such as K Q x (after winning the first round he would be end-played). There is a better line, though.

Win with the ace of spades, draw trumps, finishing in the dummy, then lead a diamond to the ace. Suppose for the moment that West plays low on this trick. You eliminate the black suits and play a diamond, won by West's queen (East fuming meanwhile). Now West will have to concede a ruff-and-discard.

As you see, West can beat the contract by playing the queen of diamonds under declarer's ace. Indeed there is every indication that he should do so; the way the play has gone, South is clearly trying to avoid two diamond losers.

Even when it is not possible to eliminate one of the side suits completely you may still be able to end-play one of the defenders.

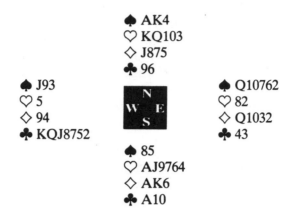

```
              ♠ AK4
              ♡ KQ103
              ◇ J875
              ♣ 96
♠ J93                        ♠ Q10762
♡ 5          N               ♡ 82
◇ 94       W   E             ◇ Q1032
♣ KQJ8752    S               ♣ 43
              ♠ 85
              ♡ AJ9764
              ◇ AK6
              ♣ A10
```

After West has opened three clubs South arrives in six hearts. He wins the club lead with the ace, draws trumps and eliminates the spades. Prospects are now in fact quite good. West has shown four cards in the majors; if he has the expected seven cards in clubs he will hold only two diamonds. So cash ◇AK and exit in clubs. West will have to win and concede a ruff-and-discard.

Life is not always so easy for declarer in an elimination situation. The defenders can sometimes strike back. Here West is in danger of being thrown in at an uncomfortable moment – but he can avoid it.

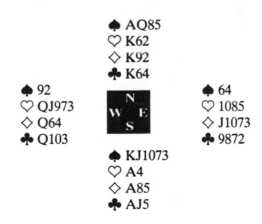

```
              ♠ AQ85
              ♡ K62
              ◇ K92
              ♣ K64
♠ 92                         ♠ 64
♡ QJ973      N               ♡ 1085
◇ Q64      W   E             ◇ J1073
♣ Q103       S               ♣ 9872
              ♠ KJ1073
              ♡ A4
              ◇ A85
              ♣ AJ5
```

West leads the queen of hearts against six spades. Declarer draws trumps, eliminates the hearts, then plays ace, king and another diamond. Suppose West follows supinely with the 4 and the 6 on the first two rounds of diamonds. He will then have to win the third round, leaving him with no safe exit. West should unblock the queen on the first or second round, allowing his partner to win the third round. The play can hardly cost a trick; if declarer had held A J x in diamonds he would doubtless have taken a finesse in the suit.

Sometimes a defender may need to unblock two cards. Suppose in the last hand the diamond position had been this:

$$\diamondsuit \text{ K92}$$
$$\diamondsuit \text{ QJ4} \qquad\qquad \diamondsuit \text{ 10763}$$
$$\diamondsuit \text{ A85}$$

Now West needs to play one honour under the ace, another under the king; East can then win the third round with the 10. It would be smart play for declarer to play at least one diamond honour at an early stage, before the defenders were alerted to a possible end-play.

On the occasions when you cannot avoid being thrown in you may have to consider your exit card carefully. Suppose you are West and have to open this suit:

$$\spadesuit \text{ AJ5}$$
$$\spadesuit \text{ K1063} \qquad\qquad \spadesuit \text{ Q82}$$
$$\spadesuit \text{ 974}$$

If declarer has the queen you are sunk, so you can place partner with this card. Declarer may have the 9, though. If you exit with a low card and declarer plays dummy's 5, your partner will have to play the queen and declarer will score two tricks. Neither is the 10 quite good enough; this will be covered by the jack and queen and partner will now have to lead away from the 8, giving declarer a chance to guess right. Only the king gives nothing away.

What do you make of this lay-out:

$\heartsuit$ A104

$\heartsuit$ Q85 $\heartsuit$ J763

$\heartsuit$ K92

If West has to open the suit a low card will not trouble declarer. The queen does at least give declarer a losing option. He may decide to win with the king, playing you for the missing honour. Similarly, of course, lead the jack from J x x.

Sometimes the best option when thrown in is to concede a ruff-and-discard. You will need to count declarer's hand to know if this is the case.

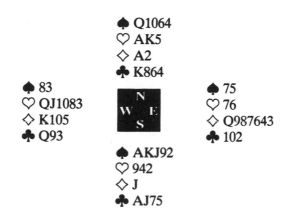

                     $\spadesuit$ Q1064

                     $\heartsuit$ AK5

                     $\diamondsuit$ A2

                     $\clubsuit$ K864

$\spadesuit$ 83 $\spadesuit$ 75

$\heartsuit$ QJ1083 $\heartsuit$ 76

$\diamondsuit$ K105 $\diamondsuit$ Q987643

$\clubsuit$ Q93 $\clubsuit$ 102

                     $\spadesuit$ AKJ92

                     $\heartsuit$ 942

                     $\diamondsuit$ J

                     $\clubsuit$ AJ75

South plays in six spades and you lead the queen of hearts, taken by the ace. Declarer draws trumps in two rounds, plays the ace of diamonds and ruffs a diamond. He now plays king and another heart, leaving you on lead in this end position:

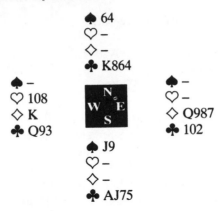

You can count declarer for five spades, three hearts and one diamond, leaving him with four clubs. So give him a ruff-and-discard, it won't help him.

10

Blocking and Unblocking

In the Culbertson–Lenz match of 1931 (don't say 'What was that?' because in publicity terms it was by far the biggest event in bridge history) there was a deal where Sidney Lenz was the declarer in 3NT and the suit led was distributed like this:

$$\clubsuit \text{ A105}$$
$$\clubsuit \text{ J9643} \qquad \clubsuit \text{ K87}$$
$$\clubsuit \text{ Q2}$$

Dummy was short of entries and when the 4 was led and East played the king Lenz unblocked the queen so that he would be able to finesse dummy's 10 on the next round. Newspapers and radio reporters all over the world made a story of this play; quite rightly, because in those days the range of blocking and unblocking plays had not been explored. We begin here with a few that occur within a single suit.

Plays to prevent the run of the suit led

The general aim here is to take your stopper earlier than necessary, leaving the defenders' remaining cards blocked.

$$\heartsuit \text{ J74}$$
$$\heartsuit \text{ K10653} \qquad \heartsuit \text{ Q9}$$
$$\heartsuit \text{ A82}$$

West leads the 5 against a notrump contract; dummy plays low, and East inserts the 9.

You can't be absolutely sure, but on balance you should win with the ace. This will be wrong only when West has led low from K Q x x x; it is unlikely that he will have led low from K Q 10 x x. You can see what will happen if you hold up; West will overtake his partner's queen on the next round and clear the suit.

Sometimes the same sort of blocking play may be advisable when you hold just 10 x x opposite the ace

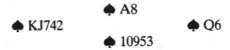

$\diamond$ 1042

$\diamond$ Q9765 $\diamond$ KJ

$\diamond$ A83

You are in 3NT and West leads the 6 to East's king. You have to force out an ace, which may be on either side. Since players with Q J 9 x x normally lead the queen, you have to choose whether to play East for K 9, in which case you should hold up (and hope that East has the missing ace), or for K–J. Playing for this latter holding is a better prospect, since you then don't mind who has the missing ace.

♠ A8

♠ KJ742   ♠ Q6

♠ 10953

When West leads the 4 it is plain that you must go up with the ace to prevent an easy run of the suit. When the 4-card holding is slightly less strong, 10 x x x or 9 x x x, the immediate play of the ace is still likely to be your best chance. For example:

♣ A5

♣ K10832   ♣ QJ

♣ 9764

West leads the 3. If you play low from dummy you are doomed unless you can run quickly for home, or unless West has no entry card. If you go up with the ace you will enjoy at least a temporary reprieve, whoever wins the first defensive trick.

This situation is tricky:

$$\heartsuit\ 72$$
$$\heartsuit\ A9653 \qquad\qquad \heartsuit\ KJ10$$
$$\heartsuit\ Q84$$

West leads the 5 to the king and East returns the jack. It will pay you to duck only if West has a six-card suit, and this is impossible unless he has led fifth best. Your best chance is to cover the jack with the queen, which in this case blocks the run of the suit.

Different considerations apply when East is known to have length in the suit. This is a well known situation:

$$\diamondsuit\ 74$$
$$\diamondsuit\ Q52 \qquad\qquad \diamondsuit\ A10983$$
$$\diamondsuit\ KJ6$$

West leads the 2 to the ace and East returns the 10. The lead of the 2 proclaims an honour, so declarer should rise with the king. This is a variation:

$$\spadesuit\ 5$$
$$\spadesuit\ J84 \qquad\qquad \spadesuit\ AK972$$
$$\spadesuit\ Q1063$$

West leads low to the king and East, who is marked with most of the defensive strength, returns the 7. Now the queen from South will block the run of the suit when the opponents next gain the lead.

Unblocking to improve your own entry situation

There are many occasions when you will have to unblock a high card to improve your own entry situation. Imagine a deal like this:

```
              ♠ Q942
              ♡ J93
              ◇ Q96
              ♣ J74
♠ K85                        ♠ J106
♡ Q7642      N               ♡ A85
◇ 73       W   E             ◇ K842
♣ Q86        S               ♣ 1095
              ♠ A73
              ♡ K10
              ◇ AJ105
              ♣ AK32
```

You are in 3NT and West leads ♡6. East wins and returns the 8. If you have to win with the king you will have no quick entry to dummy (to take the diamond finesse); you may have to make the rather desperate play of the ace and king of clubs, hoping to bring down a doubleton queen.

Looking ahead, you must drop the king of hearts under the ace. West will probably duck the next round, so you overtake the 10 with the jack and lead the 9 of diamonds (not the queen, because East might play low and you would not be able to run four tricks).

After four winning diamonds you will still have only eight tricks on top, but West will not be happily placed. He can spare one spade but the next discard will be a killer. If he throws a heart it will be safe for you to establish a second spade trick; if he throws one of his black-suit guards you will have a ninth trick there.

Sometimes you can conjure an extra entry to dummy by playing a higher card than necessary from your own hand. This type of deal happens quite often:

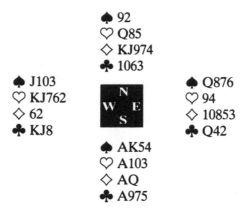

♠ 92
♡ Q85
◇ KJ974
♣ 1063

♠ J103
♡ KJ762
◇ 62
♣ KJ8

♠ Q876
♡ 94
◇ 10853
♣ Q42

♠ AK54
♡ A103
◇ AQ
♣ A975

West leads ♡6 against 3NT and East plays the 9. Suppose you win cheaply with the 10; what now? You need to bring in the diamond suit, so you will probably cash the ace and queen, overtaking with dummy's king. No luck. The 10 fails to drop on the next round and you will go one down.

You can tell from the Rule of Eleven that West holds the king of hearts. See what happens if you win the first trick with an unnecessarily high card, the ace. You now cash the ace and queen of diamonds and lead a heart towards dummy's queen. An easy ten tricks are yours.

This is a similar position in the suit led:

♣ J52

♣ Q9764

♣ 8

♣ AK103

West leads the 6 and East plays the 8. If you are short of entries to the table it may be right to win with the king. You can then establish an entry to dummy by leading towards the jack.

Sometimes you cannot reach dummy enough times under your own steam; you have to enlist help from the defenders.

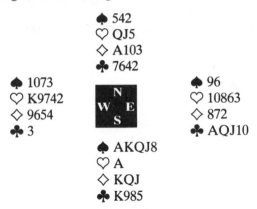

You come to a halt in four spades and West leads his singleton club. East wins with the ace and returns the queen, covered and ruffed. West exits with a trump, won in the South hand, and declarer draws trumps in two more rounds. The best chance of avoiding two further club losers is to make use of dummy's ♡ Q J, but you have only one entry to dummy, the ace of diamonds.

Wait a moment, though. How about cashing the heart ace, crossing to dummy on the second round of diamonds, and throwing your last diamond on the queen of hearts? West can look all round the room, but he won't find a way to avoid giving dummy two tricks with ♡J and ◇10.

High cards are often obstructive

High cards are usually a blessing; occasionally, though, they can get in the way. You may have to play a suit like this:

♡ K104

♡7   ♡ J863

♡ AQ952

Suppose you start with the ace, playing the 4 from dummy. West shows out when you continue with a low card to the king but now dummy's 10 blocks the run of the suit. East will not cover the 10 and you will be left, perhaps inconveniently, in the North hand. It's better to unblock the 10 on the first round, under the ace. Now you can cross to the king and finesse the 9 on the way back.

$\diamondsuit$ J1084

$\diamondsuit$ Q6 $\diamondsuit$ 93

$\diamondsuit$ AK752

Here you cash the ace and king, hoping to drop the queen. The queen does fall, good, but did you remember to throw two of the higher clubs from dummy, retaining the 4? If not, the suit will be blocked; unless you have a side entry to the South hand you will not be able to run five tricks in the suit.

When unblocking the high cards in the short holding is not possible you may need to discard them. Declarer played well on this deal.

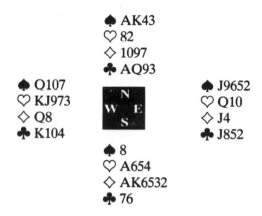

$\spadesuit$ AK43
$\heartsuit$ 82
$\diamondsuit$ 1097
$\clubsuit$ AQ93

$\spadesuit$ Q107
$\heartsuit$ KJ973
$\diamondsuit$ Q8
$\clubsuit$ K104

$\spadesuit$ J9652
$\heartsuit$ Q10
$\diamondsuit$ J4
$\clubsuit$ J852

$\spadesuit$ 8
$\heartsuit$ A654
$\diamondsuit$ AK6532
$\clubsuit$ 76

South opened 1$\diamondsuit$, West overcalled 1$\heartsuit$, and South ended in 3NT. The heart lead went to the queen, ducked by declarer, and back came a second heart. Declarer saw that a 2–2 diamond break would not be enough to give him the contract; dummy's third diamond would block the run of the suit. So, declarer held up the heart ace for one more round. West overtook his partner's $\heartsuit$10 with the jack and cleared the suit. On this third round of hearts declarer threw one of the blocking diamonds from dummy. When the diamond suit did prove to be 2–2 there was no further problem.

Defenders, too, can create entries to their partner's hand by unblocking high cards. It is declarer's job to prevent them from doing so. Look at this suit:

♠ AK63

♠ Q85   ♠ J97

♠ 1042

Suppose you need three tricks from this suit and cannot afford to let East gain the lead. You start with a low card to the ace. It will do West no good to go in with the queen; you would let this card win. If you were to cash the king on the next round West would gratefully dispose of his queen. To prevent this you must return to the South hand and lead *towards* dummy's king. West is now helpless; his queen will win the second or third round.

There are many similar situations.

♣ Q10763

♣ K5   ♣ J92

♣ A84

Again you need to keep East off lead. If you start with the ace any reasonably bright West will sacrifice the king. So, start with a low card to the queen; then, of course, you duck the next round to West.

♡ A10542

♡ Q6   ♡ J98

♡ K73

Similarly, you cannot afford to start with the king; West will ditch the queen. Play low to the ace and duck the return.

A situation much exploited by problem setters is one where by discarding a high card you can create an extra entry to the hand opposite. If you haven't seen the type before you could spend quite a while deciding how to make 6NT here:

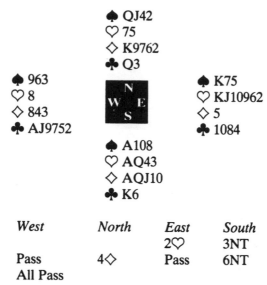

♠ QJ42
♡ 75
♢ K9762
♣ Q3

♠ 963   ♠ K75
♡ 8   ♡ KJ10962
♢ 843   ♢ 5
♣ AJ9752   ♣ 1084

♠ A108
♡ AQ43
♢ AQJ10
♣ K6

West	North	East	South
		2♡	3NT
Pass	4♢	Pass	6NT
All Pass			

Against 6NT West led ♡8, which ran to the 9 and queen. Declarer could count seven tricks in the red suits and one from clubs; he therefore needed four tricks in spades. The diamond king could be used to take the spade finesse but there was no further entry to enjoy the long spade.

Declarer cashed three diamonds in the South hand and overtook the fourth round. The queen of spades was run successfully, then declarer sprung a surprise, at any rate on his partner; he cashed the fifth round of diamonds, discarding the club king. Next came a spade to the 10, followed by the ace of spades. These cards remained:

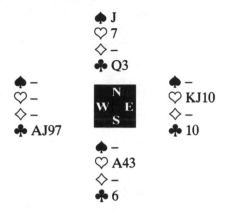

Declarer now cashed ♡A and led a club, winning the last two tricks with ♣Q and ♠J. Of course declarer was assisted by the bidding. Once East had shown up with seven points in the majors he could not hold the club ace as well. Note also that the same play would succeed if the ace and king of clubs were exchanged; declarer, now in possession of the ace of clubs, would throw it on the fifth diamond.

11

Fighting for Trump Control

When declarer's trump holding is not of the strongest he may need to take special steps to prevent losing control. Often he will make good use of the trumps in the short hand.

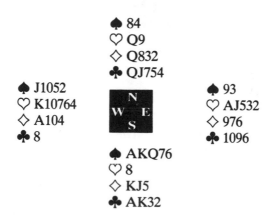

```
              ♠ 84
              ♡ Q9
              ◇ Q832
              ♣ QJ754
♠ J1052                        ♠ 93
♡ K10764                       ♡ AJ532
◇ A104                         ◇ 976
♣ 8                            ♣ 1096
              ♠ AKQ76
              ♡ 8
              ◇ KJ5
              ♣ AK32
```

South plays in four spades and West must find a lead. Since he holds four trumps he decides to attack in hearts, his own longest suit, aiming to exert pressure on declarer's trump holding. The defenders play two rounds of the suit and declarer ruffs in the South hand.

What will happen now if declarer plays three rounds of trumps? He will have lost control of the hand. If he switches to diamonds, West will win, draw declarer's last trump and cash several hearts. If instead declarer plays on clubs West will ruff the fourth round and force declarer's last trump with another heart. When West comes on lead with the diamond ace he will have two hearts to cash.

The solution on this hand is simple. Declarer must knock out the ace of diamonds before drawing trumps. Dummy's meagre trump holding will then protect him against a heart continuation. You may think that playing on diamonds risks an adverse ruff in the suit. This is true, but it won't be fatal unless the player who ruffs has only a doubleton trump.

When you can afford to lose a trick in trumps it may be wise to surrender it while dummy's trumps can still protect you from a force.

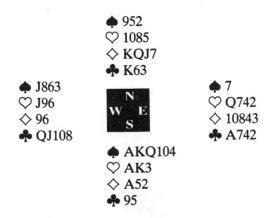

♠ 952
♥ 1085
♦ KQJ7
♣ K63

♠ J863　　　　　　　♠ 7
♥ J96　　　　　　　　♥ Q742
♦ 96　　　　　　　　　♦ 10843
♣ QJ108　　　　　　　♣ A742

♠ AKQ104
♥ AK3
♦ A52
♣ 95

Again South is in four spades. The defenders attack in clubs and declarer ruffs the third round. It may seem natural to cash two rounds of trumps now, but see what happens in that case. If you proceed to draw a third round, West will ruff the third diamond and force you with his last club; then, since you have no further entry to dummy, you will have to lose a heart trick. Nor is it any better to play on diamonds after two rounds of trumps. West will ruff the third diamond low and return the jack of trumps; again you will lose a heart.

The solution is simple, once you see it. The least complicated play is to lead the 10 of trumps from the South hand at trick four. No problem if the defenders win and play a fourth round of clubs; dummy's 9 of trumps will take care of it.

The situation on the next deal is slightly different.

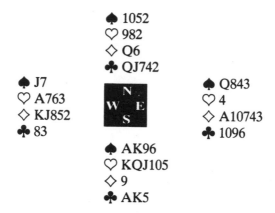

♠ 1052
♡ 982
◇ Q6
♣ QJ742

♠ J7
♡ A763
◇ KJ852
♣ 83

♠ Q843
♡ 4
◇ A10743
♣ 1096

♠ AK96
♡ KQJ105
◇ 9
♣ AK5

You reach four hearts and West (you've guessed it) starts a forcing game by leading a diamond. You ruff the second round of diamonds. What now?

The answer is that you're going down. If you play on trumps now, West will hold up his ace for two rounds. You cannot play a third round of trumps because West will win and force out your last trump with another diamond. Nor is playing on clubs any better. West will ruff the third round, notching the second trick for his side, and you will still have to lose the ace of trumps and a spade.

Your predicament is the same as on the previous hand, but the solution is different. Go back to trick 2. If instead of ruffing the second diamond you discard a spade, all will be well. A further round of diamonds can be ruffed in the dummy, so West will have to turn his attack elsewhere. It will then be safe for you to draw trumps.

It is sometimes possible to retain control by abandoning the trump suit and turning to a long side suit. This is a relatively straightforward example:

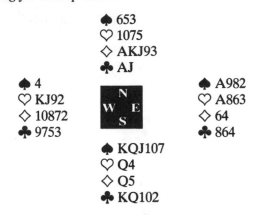

♠ 653
♡ 1075
◇ AKJ93
♣ AJ

♠ 4
♡ KJ92
◇ 10872
♣ 9753

♠ A982
♡ A863
◇ 64
♣ 864

♠ KQJ107
♡ Q4
◇ Q5
♣ KQ102

West did not hold long trumps himself on this occasion but he had some reason to think that his partner might hold four spades. He started brightly with ♡2 and the defenders continued the suit, declarer ruffing the third round. Declarer played two rounds of trumps, West showing out on the second round and East holding up the ace. A third round of trumps would allow East to take and strike back with a fourth heart; so, what could be done?

From the fall of the cards it seemed to declarer that hearts were 4–4. In that case East would hold only five cards in the minors and would ruff at some stage if declarer simply attempted to cash six winners in the minor suits. The only hope was to run good diamonds through East. After two rounds of diamonds this was the position:

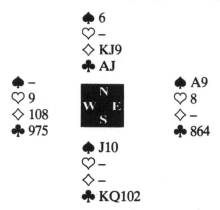

♠ 6
♡ –
♢ KJ9
♣ AJ

♠ –　　　♠ A9
♡ 9　　　♡ 8
♢ 108　　♢ –
♣ 975　　♣ 864

♠ J10
♡ –
♢ –
♣ KQ102

When another diamond was led East could see there was no future in ruffing low; declarer would overruff and cash further good cards in the minors. East decided to throw a club and declarer did the same.

To lead two more diamonds immediately would not be a good idea; East would throw both his remaining clubs and be able to ruff when a club was played. Declarer therefore cashed one club first (leaving himself with two clubs, the same as the number of diamonds in dummy). Now East had no answer when diamonds were continued.

12

Pressure in the End Game

Perhaps you have heard players learnedly discussing squeezes and have concluded that such performances are out of your league. There is no reason to think that. Complicated situations sometimes arise, but there is nothing difficult about a hand of this type:

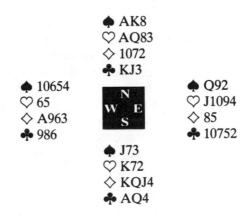

♠ AK8
♥ AQ83
♦ 1072
♣ KJ3

♠ 10654
♥ 65
♦ A963
♣ 986

♠ Q92
♥ J1094
♦ 85
♣ 10752

♠ J73
♥ K72
♦ KQJ4
♣ AQ4

South plays in 6NT and West leads ♣9. Declarer can count eleven tricks once he has cleared the diamonds. What are the chances for a twelfth trick? Hearts may be 3–3; perhaps the queen of spades will fall in two rounds. There is one other possibility: if the same player holds the queen of spades and the long hearts it should be possible to squeeze him (in other words, to force him to throw one of his guards).

See how the play develops. Declarer wins the club lead in dummy and forces out the ace of diamonds. He then cashes the two top spades. The queen does not fall but the jack is now established as a one-card menace, a card that will act as a threat against the defender holding the queen. Declarer cashes the ace and king of hearts, followed by the remaining winners in the minor suits. This is the end position:

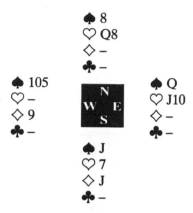

South now plays the jack of diamonds, throwing the spade from dummy. On this trick East is squeezed; he has to unguard one of the majors and declarer scores a twelfth trick.

Why did this happen? Because East could not retain in one hand as many vital cards as declarer could in two – his own and the dummy.

The end position that arose contains elements that are present in almost every squeeze:

(1) the squeeze card ($\diamondsuit$J) – the card that forces a defender to unguard a suit.

(2) a one-card menace ($\spadesuit$J) – one of the threats that the defender needs to guard.

(3) a two-card menace ($\heartsuit$Q8) – which you hope will lie against the same opponent who controls the one-card menace.

Another, almost invisible, element was present – good timing. *When declarer played the squeeze card he was in a position to win all the remaining tricks but one.* As a result, East had no card to spare when the squeeze card was played.

Rectifying the count

The deal below is similar to the first one we saw but it was misplayed when it occurred at the table. Declarer did not appreciate the need for good timing.

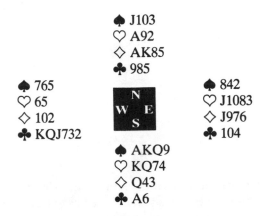

```
                    ♠ J103
                    ♡ A92
                    ◇ AK85
                    ♣ 985
  ♠ 765          ┌─────────┐          ♠ 842
  ♡ 65          │    N    │          ♡ J1083
  ◇ 102         │ W     E │          ◇ J976
  ♣ KQJ732       │    S    │          ♣ 104
                └─────────┘
                    ♠ AKQ9
                    ♡ KQ74
                    ◇ Q43
                    ♣ A6
```

South played in 6NT and West led the king of clubs. South won with the ace and tested the heart suit, finding it 4–2. With the vague idea of effecting a squeeze he now cashed four rounds of spades. This was the end position:

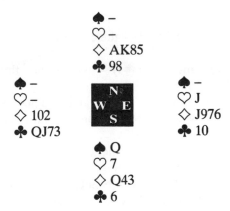

```
                    ♠ –
                    ♡ –
                    ◇ AK85
                    ♣ 98
  ♠ –            ┌─────────┐          ♠ –
  ♡ –            │    N    │          ♡ J
  ◇ 102         │ W     E │          ◇ J976
  ♣ QJ73         │    S    │          ♣ 10
                └─────────┘
                    ♠ Q
                    ♡ 7
                    ◇ Q43
                    ♣ 6
```

East did hold the sole guard in both red suits but he was under no pressure when the last spade was cashed; he had a club to throw. All declarer could do now was hope for a 3–3 diamond break. East turned up with four diamonds and the slam was one down. 'No luck,' remarked the declarer.

Not much skill, either. The hand plays very simply if South concedes a trick early in the play. You remember what we said above? Declarer should aim for the position where he can score all the remaining tricks but one. So, 'rectify the count', as the pundits say, by letting West's king of clubs win the first trick. Then the position at the end will be:

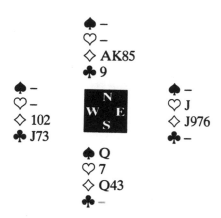

The situation is now 'tight'; East has no good discard when ♠Q is played. You see how giving up the first trick improved the timing.

Suppose you have eight top tricks in a 3NT contract and are hoping to squeeze a ninth. It is likely to help if you can lose *four* tricks at an early stage. That's what happens on the next deal.

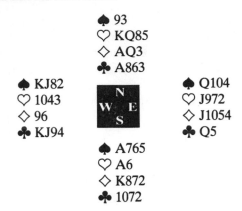

```
            ♠ 93
            ♡ KQ85
            ◇ AQ3
            ♣ A863
♠ KJ82                    ♠ Q104
♡ 1043        N          ♡ J972
◇ 96       W     E       ◇ J1054
♣ KJ94        S          ♣ Q5
            ♠ A765
            ♡ A6
            ◇ K872
            ♣ 1072
```

West leads ♠2 against 3NT and declarer sees that he has eight tricks ready to go. A ninth will be easy if the diamonds break 3–3. Failing that, various squeeze chances may arise.

The natural line of play is to duck two spades, win the third, and duck a club. If West wins this club and cashes a spade you will have reached the desired position where you have lost four tricks. If instead East wins the club and switches to, say, a heart, you must win and give up the fourth spade. However it goes, you can establish the position where East will need to control the fourth round of both diamonds and hearts, a feat that will prove beyond him.

Isolating the guard

So much for rectifying the count. Some squeeze hands require a different type of preparation.

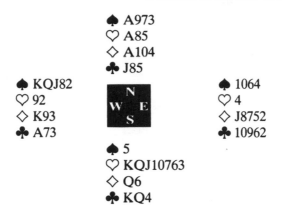

♠ A973
♡ A85
◇ A104
♣ J85

♠ KQJ82   ♠ 1064
♡ 92   ♡ 4
◇ K93   ◇ J8752
♣ A73   ♣ 10962

♠ 5
♡ KQJ10763
◇ Q6
♣ KQ4

South is in six hearts and West, who overcalled in spades, leads a high spade. Prospects are not bright, but declarer sees that if he can ruff two of dummy's spades he may, in the jargon, establish dummy's fourth spade as a one-card menace against West. (If both opponents can control spades the suit will be of no value for squeeze purposes.) You hope to find West, who has overcalled, with both long spades and the king of diamonds.

South begins by ruffing a spade at trick 2; he then draws trumps and plays on clubs. West wins the ace and returns a club. Declarer now crosses to ♡8 to ruff the third round of spades. At this stage only West guards the spades; declarer has completed a manoeuvre known as isolating the guard. Finally declarer runs his splendid trump suit, arriving at this ending:

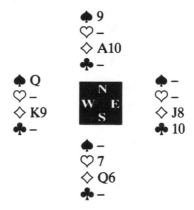

The last trump brings about what is known as a one-way or positional squeeze. West is squeezed because he has to discard *before* the dummy.

Squeeze without the count

We mentioned earlier that most squeezes occur when declarer is able to win all the remaining tricks but one. It doesn't always happen like that, though.

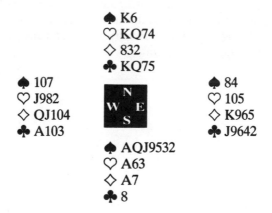

South plays in six spades and West leads ◇Q. With an ace out against him, declarer has to win and draw trumps. He then cashes the king and ace of hearts, the 10 falling from East, and proceeds to run the trump suit. This puts West on the rack somewhat. He has to find a discard in this end position:

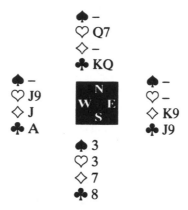

```
              ♠ –
              ♡ Q7
              ◇ –
              ♣ KQ
♠ –                        ♠ –
♡ J9          N            ♡ –
◇ J         W   E          ◇ K9
♣ A           S            ♣ J9
              ♠ 3
              ♡ 3
              ◇ 7
              ♣ 8
```

A club or a heart on the last trump would be immediately fatal, so West releases his last diamond. The spotlight now returns to declarer, who must guess how the cards lie. If hearts have been 3–3 all along he must discard a club from dummy and cash the last two hearts. However, it wouldn't take a clairvoyant to tell from West's sequence of discards that he is likely to hold a heart guard and the ace of clubs. So declarer throws a heart from dummy, then establishes a twelfth trick in clubs.

An ending of this type, where declarer concedes a trick *after* the squeeze has taken effect, is known as a squeeze without the count. That's because at the time the squeeze card is led declarer has all the tricks except two, rather than all but one.

Summary

There is much more we could say about squeeze play. There are double squeezes, triple squeezes, one-suit squeezes, criss-cross squeezes, trump squeezes, and a host of special situations. However, it takes time to master all that. One thing you will have learned is that you should never be afraid to play your last trump. At notrumps, too, it is surprising how often running your long suit will put a defender in difficulties, sometimes real, sometimes imagined. It may be a confusing subject at first, but one day, quite suddenly . . . the light will dawn.

13

Conventions in the Play

In chapter 5 we looked at opening leads and in chapter 7 at the basic signals and discards the defenders use to keep each other informed during the play. There are many variations in both these fields, though, and here – in alphabetical order – we will assess some of the more popular methods that you may encounter.

ACE FROM ACE–KING

As a rule, rubber bridge players lead the king from ace–king, tournament players the ace. There is a small weakness in either scheme. If the king is led both from A K x x and from K Q 10 x, then a partner with J x x will be uncertain whether or not to encourage. Similarly, if your method is to lead the ace from A K x x, then on the occasions when you lead the ace from A x x x partner's signal may be based on a false premise.

Assessment: This is an area where players who for many years have followed one scheme or the other are usually reluctant to change their ways. It may be that if the ace is led from A x x x and partner encourages with Q x x, it won't make much difference. The damage, when declarer holds the king, is already done.

ATTITUDE LEADS

The idea behind Attitude leads is that the more you expect to rely on the suit you are leading, the lower the card you choose. So, leading from A Q 7 4 3 against a no-trump contract you would lead the 3; from a suit such as J 7 6 4 3 you would imply less certainty by choosing the 6. You will also take into account whether you might welcome a switch by partner to another suit.

Assessment: This is a sound idea, providing more scope for judgement rather than simply producing the fourth best.

DISTRIBUTIONAL SIGNALS

When declarer plays on a suit, particularly a long suit in an entryless dummy, it may be essential for the defenders to signal their length to one another. Traditionally a high card indicates an even number of cards in the suit, a low card an odd number.

◇ KJ10962

◇ 8543   ◇ A7

◇ Q

South leads the queen towards an entryless dummy and overtakes with the king. East must take note of his partner's 8 (a high card indicating an even number of cards) and take his ace immediately. West would have played the 3 from 853 and East would then have held up the ace.

Some players use distributional signals even on partner's leads.

♡ A94

♡ QJ102   ♡ K73

♡ 865

Against a suit contract West leads the queen, won by dummy's ace. Playing natural signals, East would encourage by playing a high card, the 7. Playing distributional signals, East would play the 3, showing an odd number of cards in the suit but giving partner no clue as to the whereabouts of the king.

Assessment: All good players use distributional signals on declarer's suits to some extent. Most prefer to signal only when partner has a direct interest in the count of that suit (for example, in the entryless dummy situation); others signal throughout, trusting that the information will be of more use to partner than to declarer.

To show distribution on partner's leads, dispensing with encourage/discourage signals, seems a dubious proposition.

JOURNALIST LEADS

This term describes a system of leads first practised in the Scandinavian countries. This is the scheme:

(a) Against no-trumps

Ace: Usually from a long suit, this requests partner to unblock any honour he may hold, otherwise to indicate length by echoing (petering) with an even number.

King: May be from an AK or KQ combination.

Queen: A special convention proposes the king from speculative holdings such as K Q 10 x or K Q 9 x, but the queen from such as K Q 10 9 x or K Q J 9 x when you want partner to unblock or overtake as the case may be.

Jack: Denies a higher honour.

Ten: This is led from such as A J 10 x or K 10 9 x, expressly promising an honour higher than the jack.

Nine: From such as 10 9 8 x x.

Other spot-cards: Follow the style of Attitude leads; the lower the card led, the more reliance is to be placed on the suit; so, the 7 from 10 7 4 3, the 2 from K J 9 4 2.

(b) Against suit contracts

Honour cards: Lead the lower of two touching honours, the king from AK, the queen from KQ, and so on (a method known as Roman Leads).

Spot-cards: Fourth best from a holding including an honour, second best from low cards.

Assessment: The scheme for leads from an honour combination is certainly good. It is a weakness of conventional leads that when you lead the 10 partner cannot be sure if this a top card or from such as K 10 9 x.

NATURAL SIGNALS AND DISCARDS

The traditional scheme, both when following suit and when discarding, is that a high card is meant to encourage interest, a low card to discourage. This style is universal in the rubber bridge world and very common in tournament play.

Assessment: An occasional disadvantage of natural discards is that you may have no high card to spare in the suit you would like partner to play. You might hold K Q 2, or K Q 10 2 where you cannot afford the 10. On most hands, though, partner will have a choice of only two suits to play; you may be able to convey the intended message by discouraging in the other suit.

ODD/EVEN SIGNALS AND DISCARDS

In this method an odd-numbered card expresses encouragement, an even-number card discouragement. This applies whether you are signalling in a suit led or discarding. Sometimes, of course, you hold three odd cards and wish to discourage, or three even cards and wish to encourage. The solution then is to play your highest card, the 8 from K 8 4 2, the 9 from 9 5 3, to signal respectively approval and disapproval.

Assessment: There are times, certainly, when the generally accepted idea of playing a high card to encourage can be inconvenient. For example, with K 10 4 3 sitting over the dummy, you may not wish to spare the 10 and will be grateful that the 3 will encourage.

ROMAN LEADS, RUSINOW LEADS

Both these terms express the general idea of leading the second honour from the top, as in *Journalist Leads*.

SMITH PETERS

The idea is that when the leader's partner at no-trumps is stronger in the suit led than he is able to show at once, he will echo (peter) in the first suit played by declarer.

♣ 74

♣ J9652   ♣ KQ3

♣ A108

West leads the 5 to the queen and South wins at once because his contract is going to depend on a finesse in West's direction. If the finesse loses, West may hesitate to continue his first suit, as declarer might well have begun with ♣ A K 10. On the first round of declarer's suit East peters to assert his interest in the suit that partner led.

A second use of the Smith Peter occurs when the opening leader can see that there is no future in his first suit.

♠ 93

♠ J8742   ♠ K65

♠ AQ10

West leads the 4 to the king and ace. Declarer sets out to establish a long suit in which East has the entry card. West knows that a continuation of the first suit will not avail. If there is a possibility in another suit he echoes (peters) to convey that he does *not* want East to return the suit of the opening lead. (Note that the message is different according to which defender makes the signal.)

Assessment: This style of signalling, invented by Geoffrey Smith of Winchester, has not in general received the attention it deserves.

STRONG 10 LEADS

In this method, used only against no-trumps, the lead of a 10 guarantees at least one honour higher than the jack. The 10 would be led from K J 10 x x or Q 10 9 x x. From such as J 10 9 x the jack would be chosen; from 10 9 x, the 9.

Assessment: It is a big advantage to know whether partner has honours above the one he has led. This method has deservedly become popular in the tournament world.

SUIT PREFERENCE DISCARDS

In this method (also known as Lavinthal or McKenney) you discard from a suit in which you are *not* interested. A high discard shows interest in the higher of the other two suits, a low discard shows interest in the lower suit. So, if hearts are trumps and you are discarding from 8 5 4 2 in diamonds, you would throw the 8 to indicate an interest in spades, the 2 to show values in clubs. The 4 or 5 would be neutral cards.

Assessment: This method makes good sense because in a suit where you have no interest, such as x x x or x x x x, you will have cards to spare for signalling. This is not necessarily so in the suit where your values lie.

SUIT PREFERENCE SIGNALS

We noted in chapter 7 the type of signal that can be made when you are giving partner a ruff and wish to indicate which suit he should return. Suppose that in a suit contract your partner leads a singleton of a suit where you hold A 8 6 4 2. You win with the ace and, if you would like him to return the higher of possible suits, return the 8. The 2 would suggest interest in the lower suit.

There are many other situations where the notion of suit preference is valuable:

(a) The first suit led is of this nature:

$$\heartsuit\,8$$
$$\heartsuit\,\text{AQ9764} \qquad \heartsuit\,\text{KJ53}$$
$$\heartsuit\,102$$

West leads the ace of a suit where the defenders have bid strongly. East can suggest a switch to the higher side suit by dropping the jack, an unnecessarily high card.

The same would be true if dummy held K x instead of a singleton. East could play an abnormally high card to request a switch to the higher suit, his lowest card to suggest the lower suit. The meaning would be one of suit preference only because an attitude or count signal could hardly be of any value.

(b) Once length has been shown on one of declarer's suits, the second card may be used for suit preference.

$$\diamondsuit \text{ KJ1052}$$
$$\diamondsuit \text{ A83} \qquad\qquad \diamondsuit \text{ 964}$$
$$\diamondsuit \text{ Q7}$$

Both defenders, at no-trumps, play low on the first round to show the count. When West takes the ace on the second round the 9 from East will convey a message in favour of the higher of the alternative suits.

Assessment: Suit preference signals are universal among good players. The danger lies in overdoing them, so that a play that simply invites a continuation of the suit led (perhaps to force the dummy) may be interpreted as a suit preference signal of some kind. Signals at trick one should be interpreted as suit preference only when no other meaning is conceivable.

TRUMP ECHO

A high–low signal in the trump suit signifies an *odd* number of cards, usually three. This is different from the normal way of showing length, probably because it would often be imprudent to signal high from doubletons such as 10 x.
    Some players will always play high–low when they hold three trumps. Others prefer to reserve the signal to mean 'I have three trumps and there is a suit that I can ruff'.

Assessment: In general, it seems best to reserve the signal for occasions when there is a special message to convey, namely that partner may be able to give you a ruff.

14

Clever Tricks

Perhaps you are sometimes confronted by learned partners who favour remarks such as: 'Couldn't you have tried a Devil's Coup on that last board?' In this chapter we describe, quite briefly, a number of clever forms of play which have acquired a special name. As well as stimulating your interest in the technical side of the game, we hope that we may enable you to make a cutting reply to some over-clever partner. 'Devil's Coup, with that entry position? You must be joking!'

BATH COUP

A player of whist in the city of Bath earned much admiration when he first executed this familiar hold-up play:

$$\spadesuit\ 742$$
$$\spadesuit\ KQ105 \qquad\qquad\qquad \spadesuit\ 963$$
$$\spadesuit\ AJ8$$

West leads the king and the declarer plays low, so that the defender cannot safely continue the suit. A more sophisticated example of the play occurs in this position:

$$\diamond\ A86$$
$$\diamond\ QJ93 \qquad\qquad\qquad \diamond\ 74$$
$$\diamond\ K1052$$

West leads the queen, dummy plays low, and East plays the 4 (or the 7 if he is committed always to showing distribution). Now South false-cards with the 5 and West, in all probability, will continue the suit, having placed his partner with the 10 or king.

COUP DE L'AGONIE

This term describes the common situation where towards the end of the play the declarer scores his last trump, lower than that held by a defender, by leading a plain card towards it.

As a rule, it is the player on declarer's right who holds the winning trump, but in this example the coup is played at the expense of West.

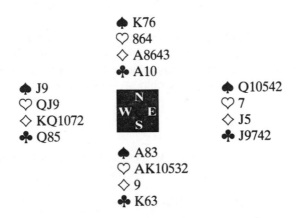

♠ K76
♡ 864
◇ A8643
♣ A10

♠ J9
♡ QJ9
◇ KQ1072
♣ Q85

♠ Q10542
♡ 7
◇ J5
♣ J9742

♠ A83
♡ AK10532
◇ 9
♣ K63

Playing in six hearts, South wins the diamond lead in dummy and, if he knows his way about, ruffs a diamond at trick two. The purpose is two-fold: he may be able to establish the diamond suit or he may be able to score four diamond ruffs in the South hand. Two top trumps reveal a loser in that suit and declarer continues his attempt to set up a long diamond. When he crosses to the ace of clubs and ruffs a second diamond, though, East shows out. It may seem that declarer must now lose a heart and a spade, but he is still alive. After king of clubs and a club ruff he ruffs dummy's fourth diamond, arriving at this position:

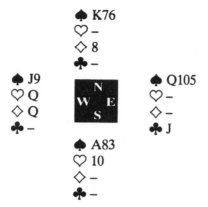

♠ K76
♡ –
◇ 8
♣ –

♠ J9　　　♠ Q105
♡ Q　　　♡ –
◇ Q　　　◇ –
♣ –　　　♣ J

♠ A83
♡ 10
◇ –
♣ –

After the ace and king of spades declarer leads dummy's last diamond. He ruffs with the 10 and West impotently follows suit. The defenders are left with two winners but only one trick on which to enjoy them!

CRISS-CROSS SQUEEZE

The majority of squeezes, as we noted in Chapter 12, contain a two-card menace headed by a winning card. Sometimes, though, the top cards are isolated, as in this position:

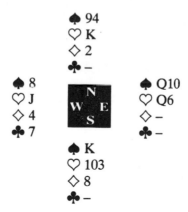

♠ 94
♡ K
◇ 2
♣ –

♠ 8　　　♠ Q10
♡ J　　　♡ Q6
◇ 4　　　◇ –
♣ 7　　　♣ –

♠ K
♡ 103
◇ 8
♣ –

South leads the winning diamond and East has no good discard. South will cash the king of whichever suit East unguards and cross to the other king to enjoy the established winner.

CROCODILE COUP

In this ending, first so named by one of the present writers, a defender has to use imagination to save his partner from being end-played.

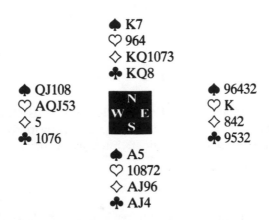

♠ K7
♡ 964
♢ KQ1073
♣ KQ8

♠ QJ108
♡ AQJ53
♢ 5
♣ 1076

♠ 96432
♡ K
♢ 842
♣ 9532

♠ A5
♡ 10872
♢ AJ96
♣ AJ4

West leads the queen of spades against five diamonds. Declarer draws trumps in three rounds, eliminates the black suits, then leads a sneaky low heart from his own hand. If West plays a low card or a middle honour, the trick will be won by East, who will have to concede a ruff-and-discard. The winning defence is for West to open his jaws like a crocodile and play the ace of hearts; he will then be able to take three tricks. Can West calculate that this is the right thing to do? He has a complete count on the hand and knows that South holds four hearts. If these include the king, there can be no defence. West must therefore assume that East holds this card.

DESCHAPELLES COUP

The strict form of this play, named after a whist champion, appears in the following example:

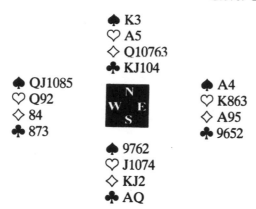

West leads ♠Q against 3NT and South, reckoning that the lead is more likely to be from Q J 10 8 x than from A Q J 10 x, plays low from dummy. East wins the next spade and must try to find an entry to his partner's hand. His best shot is to lead the king of hearts. As the cards lie, this will establish West's queen as a certain entry, whether or not declarer captures the first heart.

DEVIL'S COUP

When the defenders hold Qxx of the trump suit in one hand, Jx in the other, you might expect them to end with a trump trick. Not always! Suppose declarer can reach this ending:

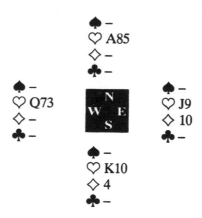

South leads $\diamond$4 and makes all three tricks. It is a rare ending, needless to say.

DOUBLE SQUEEZE

On some hands it is possible to squeeze both opponents in turn. Here the bidding and early play makes the ending not too difficult to visualise.

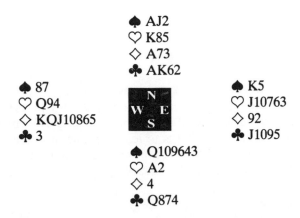

	♠ AJ2	
	♡ K85	
	♦ A73	
	♣ AK62	

♠ 87
♡ Q94
♦ KQJ10865
♣ 3

♠ K5
♡ J10763
♦ 92
♣ J1095

♠ Q109643
♡ A2
♦ 4
♣ Q874

West opens three diamonds and South arrives in six spades. He wins the diamond lead, comes to hand with a diamond ruff, and takes a losing finesse in trumps. East returns a trump and South cashes two top clubs, finding the suit unhelpfully disposed.

If declarer is a squeeze buff he may now think to himself, 'West will have to guard the diamonds, East will have to guard the clubs; no-one will be able to hold the hearts'. He plays off all the trumps and reaches this position:

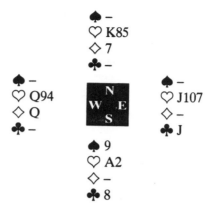

The final trump embarrasses each defender in turn. Neither can retain three hearts without establishing one of declarer's one-card menaces.

GRAND COUP

'G' coming before 'T' in the alphabet, inconveniently in this case, we look at a specialised form of the *Trump Coup* before the simpler type.

To perform a trump coup declarer often has to take ruffs in the long trump hand, to reduce his trump length to that of the defender. When the cards that he ruffs are winners the play is graced with the name *Grand Coup*. This is an example of a triple grand coup:

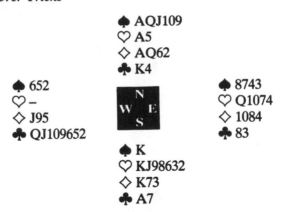

After West has opened three clubs North–South promote themselves into a grand slam in hearts. South wins the club lead with the ace and crosses to ♡A, discovering the bad news. He must now aim to reduce his trump length to match that of East. After a finesse of ♡8 he overtakes the spade king and ruffs a spade. He then plays king and another diamond, ruffs a third spade, crosses to ◇Q and ruffs a fourth spade. Then a club to the king leaves him in dummy at trick 11. East still has ♡ Q 10, but South is poised over him with ♡ K J.

INTRA-FINESSE

Brazilian maestro, Gabriel Chagas, coined this term to describe the type of play that can be made with a combination such as:

```
             ♠ Q85
♠ 106                    ♠ KJ7
             ♠ A9432
```

Suppose declarer has reason to place East with the king. He may hold the losers to one by starting with a low card to the 8 and jack; on the next round he runs the queen, pinning West's 10. This is a slightly better shot than playing East for king doubleton.

MERRIMAC COUP

The play is similar in appearance to the Deschapelles Coup but has a different objective, namely to drive out an opponent's entry. Here East sees his chance to kill a long suit in the dummy.

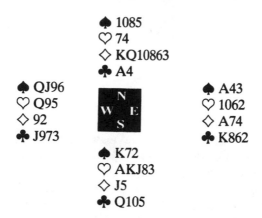

```
                    ♠ 1085
                    ♡ 74
                    ♢ KQ10863
                    ♣ A4
   ♠ QJ96                          ♠ A43
   ♡ Q95            N              ♡ 1062
   ♢ 92         W       E          ♢ A74
   ♣ J973           S              ♣ K862
                    ♠ K72
                    ♡ AKJ83
                    ♢ J5
                    ♣ Q105
```

South opens 1♡ and finishes in 3NT. When West leads ♠Q it should not be too difficult for East to win with the ace and return ♣K, dislodging dummy's ace. East will subsequently hold up ♢A for one round and declarer is held to eight tricks.

MORTON'S FORK

Cardinal Morton, who was Chancellor under King Henry VII, had a system that might well commend itself to the Inland Revenue. If a merchant lived well, obviously he had money to spare. If he lived frugally, he must have a tidy sum tucked away. Either way a heavy tax demand was in order.

That is why the term Morton's Fork is applied to this type of situation:

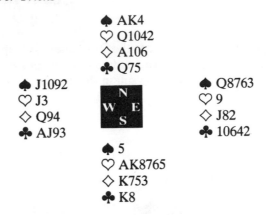

♠ AK4
♡ Q1042
◇ A106
♣ Q75

♠ J1092   ♠ Q8763
♡ J3   ♡ 9
◇ Q94   ◇ J82
♣ AJ93   ♣ 10642

♠ 5
♡ AK8765
◇ K753
♣ K8

South plays in six hearts and wins West's spade lead in the dummy. After drawing trumps declarer leads ♣8 towards dummy's queen. If West goes in with the ace declarer will have two discards for his diamond losers. If West does not go in, declarer will discard his remaining club on the spade and lose just one diamond trick. Note that declarer had to guess who held the club ace. Had East held this card, the first club lead would have to be made from dummy.

PRINCIPLE OF RESTRICTED CHOICE

This is not a 'coup' exactly, but it's a valuable guide to the best way to play various familiar combinations. Look at this holding:

◇ A1075

◇ K9843

When you lead the 3 the jack appears from West and you win with the ace. On the next round East follows with a low card. Should you play for the drop, hoping that West started with Q J, or should you finesse, playing him for a singleton jack?

It may appear that the chances are more or less equal, but this is not so. The second-round finesse is roughly twice as likely to succeed as playing for the drop. Why is this? Because on average West is

twice as likely to be dealt a singleton honour (Q or J) as to be dealt
Q J doubleton.

Look at it another way. Suppose you assume that from Q J
doubleton West would play the queen half the time, the jack the
other half. When the first finesse loses to the jack it is more likely
that West played the jack because he had to (he had a singleton jack)
than because he *chose* to do so from Q J doubleton. This form of
reasoning can be applied to a great number of combinations.

SCISSORS COUP

This expressive term describes an occasion when the declarer cuts
the communications between the defending hands, often because
they are threatening a ruff.

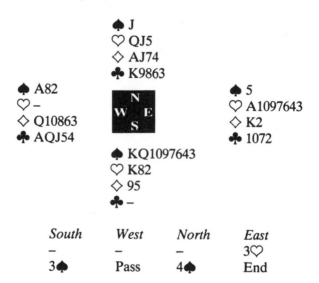

South	West	North	East
–	–	–	3♡
3♠	Pass	4♠	End

West starts with a diamond and declarer is quick to rise with
dummy's ace. What now? If he plays on trumps West will surely win
and cross to his partner's hand with a diamond to receive a heart ruff.
Instead declarer must play the king of clubs, discarding his remaining diamond. Since West has the ace of clubs, this manoeuvre

prevents East from ever gaining the lead.

STEPPING-STONE SQUEEZE

This rather pretty ending may arise when one of declarer's suits is blocked. In the 6NT contract below, declarer would have twelve tricks but for the fact that the diamond suit is blocked. West guards both the hearts and the diamonds but it is perhaps not easy to foresee the ending.

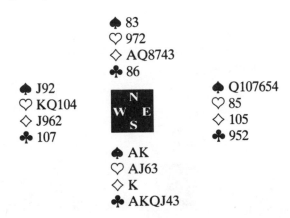

```
                    ♠ 83
                    ♡ 972
                    ◇ AQ8743
                    ♣ 86
    ♠ J92          N            ♠ Q107654
    ♡ KQ104      W   E          ♡ 85
    ◇ J962         S            ◇ 105
    ♣ 107                       ♣ 952
                    ♠ AK
                    ♡ AJ63
                    ◇ K
                    ♣ AKQJ43
```

West leads ♡K and you capture immediately, fearing a diamond switch which would cut the link with dummy. The situation may seem hopeless but look what happens when you cash your winners in the black suits.

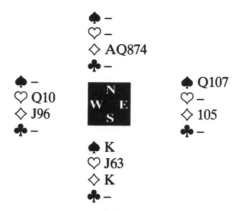

On the last spade West cannot afford another diamond or you will overtake ◇K and score three diamond tricks. He fares no better by throwing ♡10 instead, though. You can then cash ◇K and exit with a heart to West's queen. Now West has to give the last two tricks to the dummy.

The play is known as a stepping-stone squeeze because you use West's ♡Q as a means of crossing to the stranded winners in dummy.

TRUMP COUP

This form of end-play occurs when declarer cannot finesse against a defender's trump holding by straightforward play.

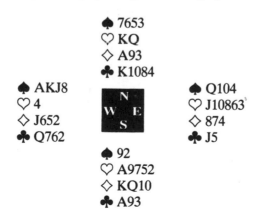

Defending against four hearts, West cashes two spades, then switches to a trump. On the next round of trumps declarer finds that East still holds J 10 8. Unperturbed, South ruffs a spade with the 7 and cashes his winners in clubs and diamonds, ending in the dummy. These cards remain:

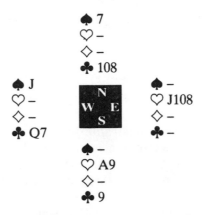

The fourth spade is led and East cannot stop declarer scoring two more tricks. (If East ruffs high South will throw the club loser.)

UPPERCUT

The term describes the familiar position when a defender ruffs his partner's lead with a high trump, forcing an even higher trump from declarer. The aim is to promote the trump holding in partner's hand.

On the following deal it is hardly evident that the defenders are destined to score three trump tricks in a diamond contract.

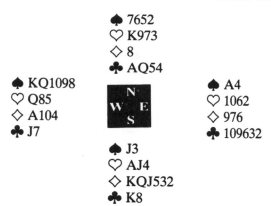

♠ 7652
♡ K973
◇ 8
♣ AQ54

♠ KQ1098
♡ Q85
◇ A104
♣ J7

♠ A4
♡ 1062
◇ 976
♣ 109632

♠ J3
♡ AJ4
◇ KQJ532
♣ K8

South is in three diamonds and West starts with ♠K, overtaken by East's ace. Two more rounds of spades follow. Even though West's third spade is a winner, East must not fail to ruff with ◇6. South overruffs, crosses to ♡K, and leads ◇8, covered by the 9, king and ace. West now plays a fourth spade, ruffed by ◇7 and overruffed. West now has ◇ 10 4 perched over South's ◇ 5 3. One down!

VIENNA COUP

This is a common form of play in preparation for a squeeze. Declarer cashes a winner in one hand to set up a secondary card in the other hand as a threat. For example, he may cash an ace to set up a queen in the other hand as a threat card. To see why this may be necessary, look at this end position:

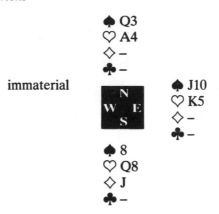

East guards both spades and hearts and you might think that playing the good diamond would squeeze him. Unfortunately it squeezes the dummy first. If ♡4 is thrown from the table East can discard ♡5 with impunity; declarer will not be able to untangle his winners.

Suppose that declarer had had the forethought to cash the ace of hearts (a Vienna Coup) before returning to the South hand to play the squeeze card. This would be the ending:

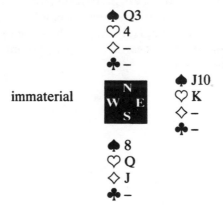

Declarer leads ◇J, throwing dummy's small heart. East is still wondering which card to throw!